A GRIEF OBSERVED READERS' EDITION

C. S. Lewis (1898–1963) was one of the intellectual giants of the twentieth century and arguably the most influential Christian writer of his day. He was a Fellow and Tutor in English Literature at Oxford University until 1954 when he was unanimously elected to the Chair of Medieval and Renaissance English at Cambridge University, a position he held until his retirement. His major contributions in literary criticism, children's literature, fantasy literature and popular theology brought him international renown and acclaim. He wrote more than thirty books, allowing him to reach a vast audience, and his works continue to attract thousands of new readers every year. His most distinguished and popular accomplishments include *The Chronicles of Narnia*, *Out of the Silent Planet*, *The Four Loves*, *The Screwtape Letters* and *Mere Christianity*.

To find out more, visit www.cslewis.com

A Grief Observed

Readers' Edition

WITH CONTRIBUTIONS FROM

Hilary Mantel
Jessica Martin
Jenna Bailey
Rowan Williams
Kate Saunders
Francis Spufford
Maureen Freely

FABER & FABER

First published in 1961
by Faber & Faber Ltd
Bloomsbury House
74–77 Great Russell Street
London WC1B 3DA
This Readers' Edition first published in 2015

Typeset by Faber & Faber Ltd
Printed and bound by CPI Group (UK) Ltd, Croydon, CRO 4YY

A CIP record for this book
is available from the British Library

ISBN 978-0-571-31087-6

Contents

A Note on the Publishing History

The text of *A Grief Observed* was sent to Faber & Faber on 27 September 1960 by the literary agency Spencer Curtis Brown, which was not at liberty to reveal the author's name (and did not want enquiries made). It was merely given as by 'Dimidius', a Latin pseudonym, implying cut in half.

It was read by T. S. Eliot and two other Faber directors. In a letter to Curtis Brown Eliot wrote, 'My wife has read it also, and we have all been deeply moved by it.' He also admitted that 'we have guessed the name of the author'. Utterly convinced that it was an exceptional work, he recommended that it be accepted for publication at a meeting of the Book Committee on 19 October 1960. The one change that Eliot proposed was a more anodyne English pseudonym, so as to dampen speculation as to the authorship. C. S. Lewis supplied Curtis Brown with a more plausible alternative and *A Grief Observed* by 'N. W. Clerk' was published by Faber in the autumn of the following year. In order to ensure specialist attention T. S. Eliot sent advance copies, together with a personal letter, to leading theologians and Church figures including the Archbishop of

Canterbury. At no point was there any clue given as to who 'N. W. Clerk' was.

The moving entry in Faber's sales catalogue in the autumn of 1961 was almost certainly written by T. S. Eliot:

A Grief Observed
N. W. Clerk

A Grief Observed is a very unusual document. It consists of a series of reflections forming a coherent whole, by a husband upon the death of his wife. A man of mature mind, a Christian, has seen a wife to whom he was deeply attached approach death by the way of a slow, painful and incurable malady. Now that she is gone, he probes his own feelings and reveals his thoughts with relentless honesty.

Several of us have read this meditation, and immediately recognised it as the work of a man of exceptional intellect, exceptional sensibility and exceptional gift of expression. The fact that we choose to publish so brief a record of sorrow is evidence enough of our belief in its value. This book will find a grateful and appreciative audience among many men and women and in particular among those who have suffered in this way and have thought, as well as felt, while they suffered.

In January 1964, following the death of C. S. Lewis, Faber decided to reissue *A Grief Observed*. A press release stated: 'When they accepted the book for publication

Fabers were aware that "N. W. Clerk" was a pseudonym; but they were not authoritatively informed until very recently that this pseudonym concealed the identity of the late Dr C. S. Lewis. The executors of Dr Lewis's estate have now given their permission for the true authorship of *A Grief Observed* to be made public.'

While the revelation of the author's name has of course added to the book's status as a classic, it has not detracted from its enduring appeal as a remarkable work of spiritual honesty in the wake of bereavement.

Robert Brown, Faber Archivist

I

A GRIEF OBSERVED

ONE

No one ever told me that grief felt so like fear. I am not afraid, but the sensation is like being afraid. The same fluttering in the stomach, the same restlessness, the yawning. I keep on swallowing.

At other times it feels like being mildly drunk, or concussed. There is a sort of invisible blanket between the world and me. I find it hard to take in what anyone says. Or perhaps, hard to want to take it in. It is so uninteresting. Yet I want the others to be about me. I dread the moments when the house is empty. If only they would talk to one another and not to me.

There are moments, most unexpectedly, when something inside me tries to assure me that I don't really mind so much, not so very much, after all. Love is not the whole of a man's life. I was happy before I ever met H. I've plenty of what are called 'resources'. People get over these things. Come, I shan't do so badly. One is ashamed to listen to this voice but it seems for a little to be making out a good case. Then comes a sudden jab of red-hot memory and all this 'commonsense' vanishes like an ant in the mouth of a furnace.

On the rebound one passes into tears and pathos.

Maudlin tears. I almost prefer the moments of agony. These are at least clean and honest. But the bath of self-pity, the wallow, the loathsome sticky-sweet pleasure of indulging it – that disgusts me. And even while I'm doing it I know it leads me to misrepresent H herself. Give that mood its head and in a few minutes I shall have substituted for the real woman a mere doll to be blubbered over. Thank God the memory of her is still too strong (will it always be too strong?) to let me get away with it.

For H wasn't like that at all. Her mind was lithe and quick and muscular as a leopard. Passion, tenderness and pain were all equally unable to disarm it. It scented the first whiff of cant or slush; then sprang, and knocked you over before you knew what was happening. How many bubbles of mine she pricked! I soon learned not to talk rot to her unless I did it for the sheer pleasure – and there's another red-hot jab – of being exposed and laughed at. I was never less silly than as H's lover.

And no one ever told me about the laziness of grief. Except at my job – where the machine seems to run on much as usual – I loathe the slightest effort. Not only writing but even reading a letter is too much. Even shaving. What does it matter now whether my cheek is rough or smooth? They say an unhappy man wants distractions – something to take him out of himself. Only as a dog-tired man wants an extra blanket on a cold night; he'd rather lie there shivering than get up and find one. It's easy to see why the lonely become untidy; finally, dirty and disgusting.

Meanwhile, where is God? This is one of the most disquieting symptoms. When you are happy, so happy that you have no sense of needing Him, so happy that you are tempted to feel His claims upon you as an interruption, if you remember yourself and turn to Him with gratitude and praise, you will be – or so it feels – welcomed with open arms. But go to Him when your need is desperate, when all other help is vain, and what do you find? A door slammed in your face, and a sound of bolting and double bolting on the inside. After that, silence. You may as well turn away. The longer you wait, the more emphatic the silence will become. There are no lights in the windows. It might be an empty house. Was it ever inhabited? It seemed so once. And that seeming was as strong as this. What can this mean? Why is He so present a commander in our time of prosperity and so very absent a help in time of trouble?

I tried to put some of these thoughts to C this afternoon. He reminded me that the same thing seems to have happened to Christ: 'Why hast thou forsaken me?' I know. Does that make it easier to understand?

Not that I am (I think) in much danger of ceasing to believe in God. The real danger is of coming to believe such dreadful things about Him. The conclusion I dread is not 'So there's no God after all,' but 'So this is what God's really like. Deceive yourself no longer.'

Our elders submitted and said 'Thy will be done.' How often had bitter resentment been stifled through sheer terror and an act of love – yes, in every sense, an act – put on to hide the operation?

Of course it's easy enough to say that God seems absent at our greatest need because He *is* absent – non-existent. But then why does He seem so present when, to put it quite frankly, we don't ask for Him?

One thing, however, marriage has done for me. I can never again believe that religion is manufactured out of our unconscious, starved desires and is a substitute for sex. For those few years H and I feasted on love; every mode of it – solemn and merry, romantic and realistic, sometimes as dramatic as a thunderstorm, sometimes as comfortable and unemphatic as putting on your soft slippers. No cranny of heart or body remained unsatisfied. If God were a substitute for love we ought to have lost all interest in Him. Who'd bother about substitutes when he has the thing itself? But that isn't what happens. We both knew we wanted something besides one another – quite a different kind of something, a quite different kind of want. You might as well say that when lovers have one another they will never want to read, or eat – or breathe.

After the death of a friend, years ago, I had for some time a most vivid feeling of certainty about his continued life; even his enhanced life. I have begged to be given even one hundredth part of the same assurance about H. There is no answer. Only the locked door, the iron curtain, the vacuum, absolute zero. 'Them as asks don't get.' I was a fool to ask. For now, even if that assurance came I should distrust it. I should think it a self-hypnosis induced by my own prayers.

At any rate I must keep clear of the spiritualists. I promised H I would. She knew something of those circles.

Keeping promises to the dead, or to anyone else, is very well. But I begin to see that 'respect for the wishes of the dead' is a trap. Yesterday I stopped myself only in time from saying about some trifle 'H wouldn't have liked that.' This is unfair to the others. I should soon be using 'what H would have liked' as an instrument of domestic tyranny; with her supposed likings becoming a thinner and thinner disguise for my own.

I cannot talk to the children about her. The moment I try, there appears on their faces neither grief, nor love, nor fear, nor pity, but the most fatal of all non-conductors, embarrassment. They look as if I were committing an indecency. They are longing for me to stop. I felt just the same after my own mother's death when my father mentioned her. I can't blame them. It's the way boys are.

I sometimes think that shame, mere awkward, sense-less shame, does as much towards preventing good acts and straightforward happiness as any of our vices can do. And not only in boyhood.

Or are the boys right? What would H herself think of this terrible little notebook to which I come back and back? Are these jottings morbid? I once read the sentence 'I lay awake all night with toothache, thinking about toothache and about lying awake.' That's true to life. Part of every misery is, so to speak, the misery's shadow or reflection: the fact that you don't merely suffer but have to keep on thinking about the fact that you suffer. I not only live each endless day in grief, but live each day thinking about living each day in grief. Do these notes merely aggravate that side of it? Merely confirm the monotonous, tread-mill march of the mind round one subject? But what am I to do? I must have some drug, and reading isn't a strong enough drug now. By writing it all down (all? – no: one thought in a hundred) I believe I get a little outside it. That's how I'd defend it to H. But ten to one she'd see a hole in the defence.

It isn't only the boys either. An odd by-product of my loss is that I'm aware of being an embarrassment to everyone I meet. At work, at the club, in the street, I see people, as they approach me, trying to make up their minds whether they'll 'say something about it' or not. I hate it if they do, and if they don't. Some funk it altogether. R has been avoiding me for a week. I like best the well brought-up young men, almost boys, who walk up to me as if I were a dentist, turn very red, get it over, and then edge away to the bar as quickly as they decently can. Perhaps the bereaved ought to be isolated in special settlements like lepers.

To some I'm worse than an embarrassment. I am a death's head. Whenever I meet a happily married pair I can feel them both thinking, 'One or other of us must some day be as he is now.'

At first I was very afraid of going to places where H and I had been happy – our favourite pub, our favourite wood. But I decided to do it at once – like sending a pilot up again as soon as possible after he's had a crash. Unexpectedly, it makes no difference. Her absence is no more emphatic in those places than anywhere else. It's not local at all. I suppose that if one were forbidden all salt one wouldn't notice it much more in any one food than in another. Eating in general would be different, every day, at every meal. It is like that. The act of living is different all through. Her absence is like the sky, spread over everything.

But no, that is not quite accurate. There is one place where her absence comes locally home to me, and it is a place I can't avoid. I mean my own body. It had such a different importance while it was the body of H's lover. Now it's like an empty house. But don't let me deceive myself. This body would become important to me again, and pretty quickly, if I thought there was anything wrong with it.

Cancer, and cancer, and cancer. My mother, my father, my wife. I wonder who is next in the queue.

Yet H herself, dying of it, and well knowing the fact, said that she had lost a great deal of her old horror at it. When the reality came, the name and the idea were in some degree disarmed. And up to a point I very nearly understood. This is important. One never meets just Cancer, or War, or Unhappiness (or Happiness). One only meets each hour or moment that comes. All manner of ups and downs. Many bad spots in our best times, many good ones in our worst. One never gets the total impact of what we call 'the thing itself'. But we call it wrongly. The thing itself is simply all these ups and downs: the rest is a name or an idea.

It is incredible how much happiness, even how much gaiety, we sometimes had together after all hope was gone. How long, how tranquilly, how nourishingly, we talked together that last night!

And yet, not quite together. There's a limit to the 'one flesh'. You can't really share someone else's weakness, or fear or pain. What you feel may be bad. It might conceivably be as bad as what the other felt, though I should distrust anyone who claimed that it was. But it would still be quite different. When I speak of fear, I mean the merely animal fear, the recoil of the organism from its destruction; the smothery feeling; the sense of being a rat in a trap. It can't be transferred. The mind can sympathize; the body, less. In one way the bodies of lovers can do it least. All their love passages have trained them to have, not identical, but complementary, correlative, even opposite, feelings about one another.

We both knew this. I had my miseries, not hers; she had hers, not mine. The end of hers would be the coming -of-age of mine. We were setting out on different roads. This cold truth, this terrible traffic-regulation ('You, Madam, to the right – you, Sir, to the left') is just the beginning of the separation which is death itself.

And this separation, I suppose, waits for all. I have been thinking of H and myself as peculiarly unfortunate in being torn apart. But presumably all lovers are. She once said to me, 'Even if we both died at exactly the same moment, as we lie here side by side, it would be just as much a separation as the one you're so afraid of.' Of course she didn't *know,* any more than I do. But she was near death; near enough to make a good shot. She used to quote 'Alone into the Alone.' She said it felt like that. And how immensely improbable that it should be otherwise! Time and space and body were the very things that brought us together; the telephone wires by which we communicated. Cut one off, or cut both off simultaneously. Either way, mustn't the conversation stop?

Unless you assume that some other means of communication – utterly different, yet doing the same work, would be immediately substituted. But then, what conceivable point could there be in serving the old ones? Is God a clown who whips away your bowl of soup one moment in order, next moment, to replace it with another bowl of the same soup? Even nature isn't such a clown as that. She never plays exactly the same tune twice.

It is hard to have patience with people who say 'There is no death' or 'Death doesn't matter'. There is death. And whatever is matters. And whatever happens has consequences, and it and they are irrevocable and irreversible. You might as well say that birth doesn't matter. I look up at the night sky. Is anything more certain than that in all those vast times and spaces, if I were allowed to search them, I should nowhere find her face, her voice, her touch? She died. She is dead. Is the word so difficult to learn?

I have no photograph of her that's any good. I cannot even see her face distinctly in my imagination. Yet the odd face of some stranger seen in a crowd this morning may come before me in vivid perfection the moment I close my eyes tonight. No doubt, the explanation is simple enough. We have seen the faces of those we know best so variously, from so many angles, in so many lights, with so many expressions – waking, sleeping, laughing, crying, eating, talking, thinking – that all the impressions crowd into our memory together and cancel out in a mere blur. But her voice is still vivid. The remembered voice – that can turn me at any moment to a whimpering child.

TWO

For the first time I have looked back and read these notes. They appal me. From the way I've been talking anyone would think that H's death mattered chiefly for its effect on myself. Her point of view seems to have dropped out of sight. Have I forgotten the moment of bitterness when she cried out 'And there was so much to live for'? Happiness had not come to her early in life. A thousand years of it would not have made her *blasée*. Her palate for all the joys of sense and intellect and spirit was fresh and unspoiled. Nothing would have been wasted on her. She liked more things and liked them more than anyone I have known. A noble hunger, long unsatisfied, met at last its proper food, and almost instantly the food was snatched away. Fate (or whatever it is) delights to produce a great capacity and then frustrate it. Beethoven went deaf. By our standards a mean joke; the monkey trick of a spiteful imbecile.

I must think more about H and less about myself.

Yes, that sounds very well. But there's a snag. I am thinking about her nearly always. Thinking of the H facts – real words, looks, laughs, and actions of hers. But it is my own mind that selects and groups them.

Already, less than a month after her death, I can feel the slow, insidious beginning of a process that will make the H I think of into a more and more imaginary woman. Founded on fact, no doubt, I shall put in nothing fictitious (or I hope I shan't). But won't the composition inevitably become more and more my own? The reality is no longer there to check me, to pull me up short, as the real H so often did, so unexpectedly, by being so thoroughly herself and not me.

The most precious gift that marriage gave me was this constant impact of something very close and intimate yet all the time unmistakably other, resistant – in a word, real. Is all that work to be undone? Is what I shall still call H to sink back horribly into being not much more than one of my old bachelor pipe-dreams? Oh my dear, my dear, come back for one moment and drive that miserable phantom away. Oh God, God, why did you take such trouble to force this creature out of its shell if it is now doomed to crawl back – to be sucked back – into it?

Today I had to meet a man I haven't seen for ten years. And all that time I had thought I was remembering him well – how he looked and spoke and the sort of things he said. The first five minutes of the real man shattered the image completely. Not that he had changed. On the contrary. I kept on thinking, 'Yes, of course, of course, I'd forgotten that he thought that – or disliked this, or knew so-and-so – or jerked his head back that way.' I had known all these things once and I recognized them the moment I met them again. But they had all faded out of my mental picture of him, and when they were all replaced by his actual presence the total effect was quite astonishingly different from the image I had carried about with me for those ten years. How can I hope that this will not happen to my memory of H? That it is not happening already? Slowly, quietly, like snow-flakes – like the small flakes that come when it is going to snow all night – little flakes of me, my impressions, my selections, are settling down on the image of her. The real shape will be quite hidden in the end. Ten minutes – ten seconds – of the real H would correct all this. And yet, even if those ten seconds were allowed me, one second later the little flakes would begin to fall again. The rough, sharp, cleansing tang of her otherness is gone.

What pitiable cant to say 'She will live forever in my memory!' *Live?* That is exactly what she won't do. You might as well think like the old Egyptians that you can keep the dead by embalming them. Will nothing persuade us that they are gone? What's left? A corpse, a memory, and (in some versions) a ghost. All mockeries or horrors. Three more ways of spelling the word *dead*. It was H I loved. As if I wanted to fall in love with my memory of her, an image in my own mind! It would be a sort of incest.

I remember being rather horrified one summer morning long ago when a burly, cheerful labouring man, carrying a hoe and a watering pot came into our churchyard, and as he pulled the gate behind him, shouted over his shoulder to two friends, 'See you later, I'm just going to visit Mum.' He meant he was going to weed and water and generally tidy up her grave. It horrified me because this mode of sentiment, all this churchyard stuff, was and is simply hateful, even inconceivable, to me. But in the light of my recent thoughts I am beginning to wonder whether, if one could take that man's line (I can't), there isn't a good deal to be said for it. A six-by-three-foot flower-bed had become Mum. That was his symbol for her, his link with her. Caring for it was visiting her. May this not be in one way better than preserving and caressing an image in one's own memory? The grave and the image are equally links with the irrecoverable and symbols for the unimaginable. But the image has the added disadvantage that it will do whatever you want. It will smile or frown, be tender, gay, ribald, or argumentative just as your mood demands. It is a puppet of which you hold the strings. Not yet of course. The reality is still too fresh; genuine and wholly involuntary memories can still, thank God, at any moment rush in and tear the strings out of my hands. But the fatal obedience of the image, its insipid dependence on me, is bound to increase. The flower-bed on the other hand is an obstinate, resistant, often intractable bit of reality, just as Mum in her lifetime doubtless was. As H was.

Or as H is. Can I honestly say that I believe she now is anything? The vast majority of the people I meet, say, at work, would certainly think she is not. Though naturally they wouldn't press the point on me. Not just now anyway. What do I really think? I have always been able to pray for the other dead, and I still do, with some confidence. But when I try to pray for H, I halt. Bewilderment and amazement come over me. I have a ghastly sense of unreality, of speaking into a vacuum about a nonentity.

The reason for the difference is only too plain. You never know how much you really believe anything until its truth or falsehood becomes a matter of life and death to you. It is easy to say you believe a rope to be strong and sound as long as you are merely using it to cord a box. But suppose you had to hang by that rope over a precipice. Wouldn't you then first discover how much you really trusted it? The same with people. For years I would have said that I had perfect confidence in BR. Then came the moment when I had to decide whether I would or would not trust him with a really important secret. That threw quite a new light on what I called my 'confidence' in him. I discovered that there was no such thing. Only a real risk tests the reality of a belief. Apparently the faith – I thought it faith – which enables me to pray for the other dead has seemed strong only because I have never really cared, not desperately, whether they existed or not. Yet I thought I did.

But there are other difficulties. 'Where is she now?' That is, *in what place* is she *at the present time.* But if H is not a body – and the body I loved is certainly no longer she – she is in no place at all. And 'the present time' is a date or point in our time series. It is as if she were on a journey without me and I said, looking at my watch, 'I wonder is she at Euston now.' But unless she is proceeding at sixty seconds a minute along this same time-line that all we living people travel by, what does *now* mean? If the dead are not in time, or not in our sort of time, is there any clear difference, when we speak of them, between *was* and *is* and *will be?*

Kind people have said to me 'She is with God.' In one sense that is most certain. She is, like God, incomprehensible and unimaginable.

But I find that this question, however important it may be in itself, is not after all very important in relation to grief. Suppose that the earthly lives she and I shared for a few years are in reality only the basis for, or prelude to, or earthly appearance of, two unimaginable, super-cosmic, eternal somethings. Those somethings could be pictured as spheres or globes. Where the plane of Nature cuts through them – that is, in earthly life –

they appear as two circles (circles are slices of spheres). Two circles that touched. But those two circles, above all the point at which they touched, are the very thing I am mourning for, homesick for, famished for. You tell me 'she goes on'. But my heart and body are crying out, come back, come back. Be a circle, touching my circle on the plane of Nature. But I know this is impossible. I know that the thing I want is exactly the thing I can never get. The old life, the jokes, the drinks, the arguments, the lovemaking, the tiny, heartbreaking commonplace. On any view whatever, to say 'H is dead', is to say 'All that is gone'. It is a part of the past. And the past is the past and that is what time means, and time itself is one more name for death, and Heaven itself is a state where 'the former things have passed away'.

Talk to me about the truth of religion and I'll listen gladly. Talk to me about the duty of religion and I'll listen submissively. But don't come talking to me about the consolations of religion or I shall suspect that you don't understand.

Unless, of course, you can literally believe all that stuff about family reunions 'on the further shore', pictured in entirely earthly terms. But that is all unscriptural, all out of bad hymns and lithographs. There's not a word of it in the Bible. And it rings false. We *know* it couldn't be like that. Reality never repeats. The exact same thing is never taken away and given back. How well the Spiritualists bait their hook! 'Things on this side are not so different after all.' There are cigars in Heaven. For that is what we should all like. The happy past restored.

And that, just that, is what I cry out for, with mad, midnight endearments and entreaties spoken into the empty air.

And poor C quotes to me 'Do not mourn like those that have no hope'. It astonishes me, the way we are invited to apply to ourselves words so obviously addressed to our betters. What St. Paul says can comfort only those who love God better than the dead, and the dead better than themselves. If a mother is mourning not for what she has lost but for what her dead child has lost, it is a comfort to believe that the child has not lost the end for which it was created. And it is a comfort to believe that she herself, in losing her chief or only natural happiness, has not lost a greater thing, that she may still hope to 'glorify God and enjoy Him forever'. A comfort to the God-aimed, eternal spirit within her. But not to her motherhood. The specifically maternal happiness must be written off. Never, in any place or time, will she have her son on her knees, or bath him, or tell him a story, or plan for his future, or see her grandchild.

They tell me H is happy now, they tell me she is at peace. What makes them so sure of this? I don't mean that I fear the worst of all. Nearly her last words were

'I am at peace with God'. She had not always been. And she never lied. And she wasn't easily deceived; least of all, in her own favour. I don't mean that. But why are they so sure that all anguish ends with death? More than half the Christian world, and millions in the East, believe otherwise. How do they know she is 'at rest'? Why should the separation (if nothing else) which so agonizes the lover who is left behind be painless to the lover who departs?

'Because she is in God's hands.' But if so, she was in God's hands all the time, and I have seen what they did to her here. Do they suddenly become gentler to us the moment we are out of the body? And if so, why? If God's goodness is inconsistent with hurting us, then either God is not good or there is no God: for in the only life we know He hurts us beyond our worst fears and beyond all we can imagine. If it is consistent with hurting us, then He may hurt us after death as unendurably as before it.

Sometimes it is hard not to say 'God forgive God'. Sometimes it is hard to say so much. But if our faith is true, He didn't. He crucified Him.

Come, what do we gain by evasions? We are under the harrow and can't escape. Reality, looked at steadily, is unbearable. And how or why did such a reality blossom (or fester) here and there into the terrible phenomenon called consciousness? Why did it produce things like us who can see it and, seeing it, recoil in loathing? Who (stranger still) want to see it and take pains to find it out, even when no need compels them and even though the sight of it makes an incurable ulcer in their hearts? People like H herself, who would have truth at any price.

If H 'is not', then she never was. I mistook a cloud of atoms for a person. There aren't, and never were, any people. Death only reveals the vacuity that was always there. What we call the living are simply those who have not yet been unmasked. All equally bankrupt, but some not yet declared.

But this must be nonsense; vacuity revealed to whom? bankruptcy declared to whom? To other boxes of fireworks or clouds of atoms. I will never believe – more strictly I can't believe – that one set of physical events could be, or make, a mistake about other sets.

No, my real fear is not of materialism. If it were true, we – or what we mistake for 'we' – could get out, get from under the harrow. An overdose of sleeping pills would do it. I am more afraid that we are really rats in a trap. Or, worse still, rats in a laboratory. Someone said, I believe, 'God always geometrizes'. Supposing the truth were 'God always vivisects'?

Sooner or later I must face the question in plain language. What reason have we, except our own desperate wishes, to believe that God is, by any standard we can conceive, 'good'? Doesn't all the *prima facie* evidence suggest exactly the opposite? What have we to set against it?

We set Christ against it. But how if He were mistaken? Almost His last words may have a perfectly clear meaning. He had found that the Being He called Father was horribly and infinitely different from what He had supposed. The trap, so long and carefully prepared and so subtly baited, was at last sprung, on the cross. The vile practical joke had succeeded.

What chokes every prayer and every hope is the memory of all the prayers H and I offered and all the false hopes we had. Not hopes raised merely by our own wishful thinking; hopes encouraged, even forced upon us, by false diagnoses, by X-ray photographs, by strange remissions, by one temporary recovery that might have ranked as a miracle. Step by step we were 'led up the garden path'. Time after time, when He seemed most gracious He was really preparing the next torture.

I wrote that last night. It was a yell rather than a thought. Let me try it over again. Is it rational to believe in a bad God? Anyway, in a God so bad as all that? The Cosmic Sadist, the spiteful imbecile?

I think it is, if nothing else, too anthropomorphic. When you come to think of it, it is far more anthropomorphic than picturing Him as a grave old king with a long beard. That image is a Jungian archetype. It links God with all the wise old kings in the fairy-tales,

with prophets, sages, magicians. Though it is (formally) the picture of a man, it suggests something more
than humanity. At the very least it gets in the idea of
something older than yourself, something that knows
more, something you can't fathom. It preserves mys-
tery. Therefore room for hope. Therefore room for a
dread or awe that needn't be mere fear of mischief from
a spiteful potentate. But the picture I was building up
last night is simply the picture of a man like SC – who
used to sit next to me at dinner and tell what he'd been
doing to the cats that afternoon. Now a being like SC,
however magnified, couldn't invent or create or govern
anything. He would set traps and try to bait them. But
he'd never have thought of baits like love, or laughter,
or daffodils, or a frosty sunset. *He* make a universe?
He couldn't make a joke, or a bow, or an apology, or a
friend.

Or could one seriously introduce the idea of a bad
God, as it were by the back door, through a sort of
extreme Calvinism? You could say we are fallen and
depraved. We are so depraved that our ideas of goodness count for nothing; or worse than nothing – the
very fact that we think something good is presumptive
evidence that it is really bad. Now God has in fact – our
worse fears are true – all the characteristics we regard
as bad: unreasonableness, vanity, vindictiveness, injus-
tice, cruelty. But all these blacks (as they seem to us) are

[26]

really whites. It's only our depravity makes them look black to us.

And so what? This, for all practical (and speculative) purposes sponges God off the slate. The word *good*, applied to Him, becomes meaningless: like abracadabra. We have no motive for obeying Him. Not even fear. It is true we have His threats and promises. But why should we believe them? If cruelty is from His point of view 'good', telling lies may be 'good' too. Even if they are true, what then? If His ideas of good are so very different from ours, what He calls 'Heaven' might well be what we should call Hell, and vice-versa. Finally, if reality at its very root is so meaningless to us – or, putting it the other way round, if we are such total imbeciles – what is the point of trying to think either about God or about anything else? This knot comes undone when you try to pull it tight.

Why do I make room in my mind for such filth and nonsense? Do I hope that if feeling disguises itself as thought I shall feel less? Aren't all these notes the senseless writhings of a man who won't accept the fact that there is nothing we can do with suffering except to suffer it? Who still thinks there is some device (if only he could find it) which will make pain not to be pain. It doesn't really matter whether you grip the arms of the dentist's chair or let your hands lie in your lap. The drill drills on.

And grief still feels like fear. Perhaps, more strictly, like suspense. Or like waiting; just hanging about waiting for something to happen. It gives life a permanently provisional feeling. It doesn't seem worth starting anything. I can't settle down. I yawn, I fidget, I smoke too much. Up till this I always had too little time. Now there is nothing but time. Almost pure time, empty successiveness.

One flesh. Or, if you prefer, one ship. The starboard engine has gone. I, the port engine, must chug along somehow till we make harbour. Or rather, till the journey ends. How can I assume a harbour? A lee shore, more likely, a black night, a deafening gale, breakers ahead – and any lights shown from the land probably being waved by wreckers. Such was H's landfall. Such was my mother's. I say their landfalls; not their arrivals.

THREE

It's not true that I'm always thinking of H. Work and conversation make that impossible. But the times when I'm not are perhaps my worst. For then, though I have forgotten the reason, there is spread over everything a vague sense of wrongness, of something amiss. Like in those dreams where nothing terrible occurs – nothing that would sound even remarkable if you told it at breakfast-time – but the atmosphere, the taste, of the whole thing is deadly. So with this. I see the rowan berries reddening and don't know for a moment why they, of all things, should be depressing. I hear a clock strike and some quality it always had before has gone out of the sound. What's wrong with the world to make it so flat, shabby, worn-out looking? Then I remember.

This is one of the things I'm afraid of. The agonies, the mad midnight moments, must, in the course of nature, die away. But what will follow? Just this apathy, this dead flatness? Will there come a time when I no longer ask why the world is like a mean street, because I shall take the squalor as normal? Does grief finally subside into boredom tinged by faint nausea?

Feelings, and feelings, and feelings. Let me try thinking instead. From the rational point of view, what new
factor has H's death introduced into the problem of the
universe? What grounds has it given me for doubting
all that I believe? I knew already that these things, and
worse, happened daily. I would have said that I had taken
them into account. I had been warned – I had warned
myself – not to reckon on worldly happiness. We were
even promised sufferings. They were part of the programme. We were even told 'Blessed are they that
mourn' and I accepted it. I've got nothing that I hadn't
bargained for. Of course it is different when the thing
happens to oneself, not to others, and in reality, not in
imagination. Yes; but should it, for a sane man, make
quite such a difference as this? No. And it wouldn't for a
man whose faith had been real faith and whose concern
for other people's sorrows had been real concern. The case
is too plain. If my house has collapsed at one blow, that
is because it was a house of cards. The faith which 'took
these things into account' was not faith but imagination.
The taking them into account was not real sympathy. If
I had really cared, as I thought I did, about the sorrows
of the world, I should not have been so overwhelmed
when my own sorrow came. It has been an imaginary
faith playing with innocuous counters labelled 'Illness',
'Pain', 'Death' and 'Loneliness'. I thought I trusted the
rope until it mattered to me whether it would bear me.

Now it matters, and I find I didn't.

Bridge-players tell me that there must be some money on the game 'or else people won't take it seriously'. Apparently it's like that. Your bid – for God or no God, for a good God or the Cosmic Sadist, for eternal life or nonentity – will not be serious if nothing much is staked on it. And you will never discover how serious it was until the stakes are raised horribly high; until you find that you are playing not for counters or for sixpences but for every penny you have in the world. Nothing less will shake a man – or at any rate a man like me – out of his merely verbal thinking and his merely notional beliefs. He has to be knocked silly before he comes to his senses. Only torture will bring out the truth. Only under torture does he discover it himself.

And I must surely admit – H would have forced me to admit in a few passes – that, if my house was a house of cards, the sooner it was knocked down the better. And only suffering could do it. But then the Cosmic Sadist and Eternal Vivisector becomes an unnecessary hypothesis.

Is this last note a sign that I'm incurable, that when reality smashes my dream to bits, I mope and snarl while the first shock lasts, and then patiently, idiotically, start putting it together again? And so always? However often the house of cards falls, shall I set about rebuilding it? Is that what I'm doing now?

Indeed it's likely enough that what I shall call, if it happens, a 'restoration of faith' will turn out to be only one more house of cards. And I shan't know whether it is or not until the next blow comes – when, say, fatal disease is diagnosed in my body too, or war breaks out, or I have ruined myself by some ghastly mistake in my work. But there are two questions here. In which sense may it be a house of cards? Because the things I am believing are only a dream, or because I only dream that I believe them?

As for the things themselves, why should the thoughts I had a week ago be any more trustworthy than the better thoughts I have now? I am surely, in general, a saner man than I was then. Why should the desperate imagining of a man dazed – I said it was like being concussed – be especially reliable?

Because there was no wishful thinking in them? Because, being so horrible, they were therefore all the more likely to be true? But there are fear-fulfilment as well as wish-fulfilment dreams. And were they wholly distasteful? No. In a way I liked them. I am even aware of a slight reluctance to accept the opposite thoughts. All that stuff about the Cosmic Sadist was not so much the expression of thought as of hatred. I was getting from it the only pleasure a man in anguish can get; the pleasure of hitting back. It was really just Billingsgate – mere abuse; 'telling God what I thought of Him'. And of course, as in all abusive language, 'what I thought' didn't mean what I thought true. Only what I thought would offend Him (and His worshippers) most. That sort of thing is never said without some pleasure. Gets it 'off your chest'. You feel better for a moment.

But the mood is no evidence. Of course the cat will growl and spit at the operator and bite him if she can. But the real question is whether he is a vet or a vivisector. Her bad language throws no light on it one way or the other.

And I can believe He is a vet when I think of my own suffering. It is harder when I think of hers. What is grief compared with physical pain? Whatever fools may say, the body can suffer twenty times more than the mind. The mind has always some power of evasion. At worst, the unbearable thought only comes back and back, but the physical pain can be absolutely continuous. Grief is like a bomber circling round and dropping its bombs each time the circle brings it overhead; physical pain is like the steady barrage on a trench in World War One, hours of it with no let-up for a moment. Thought is never static; pain often is.

What sort of a lover am I to think so much about my affliction and so much less about hers? Even the insane call, 'Come back', is all for my own sake. I never even raised the question whether such a return, if it were possible, would be good for her. I want her back as an ingredient in the restoration of *my* past. Could I have wished her anything worse? Having got once through death, to come back and then, at some later date, have all her dying to do over again? They call Stephen the first martyr. Hadn't Lazarus the rawer deal?

I begin to see. My love for H was of much the same quality as my faith in God. I won't exaggerate, though. Whether there was anything but imagination in the faith, or anything but egoism in the love, God knows. I don't. There may have been a little more; especially in my love for H. But neither was the thing I thought it was. A good deal of the card-castle about both.

What does it matter how this grief of mine evolves or what I do with it? What does it matter how I remember her or whether I remember her at all? None of these alternatives will either ease or aggravate her past anguish.

Her past anguish. How do I know that all her anguish is past? I never believed before – I thought it immensely improbable – that the faithfulest soul could leap straight into perfection and peace the moment death has rattled in the throat. It would be wishful thinking with a vengeance to take up that belief now. H was a splendid thing; a soul straight, bright, and tempered like a sword. But not a perfected saint. A sinful woman married to a sinful man; two of God's patients, not yet cured. I know there are not only tears to be dried but stains to be scoured. The sword will be made even brighter.

But oh God, tenderly, tenderly. Already, month by month and week by week you broke her body on the wheel whilst she still wore it. Is it not yet enough?

The terrible thing is that a perfectly good God is in this matter hardly less formidable than a Cosmic Sadist. The more we believe that God hurts only to heal, the less we can believe that there is any use in begging for tenderness. A cruel man might be bribed – might grow tired of his vile sport – might have a temporary fit of mercy, as alcoholics have fits of sobriety. But suppose that what you are up against is a surgeon whose intentions are wholly good. The kinder and more conscientious he is, the more inexorably he will go on cutting. If he yielded to your entreaties, if he stopped before the operation was complete, all the pain up to that point would have been useless. But is it credible that such extremities of torture should be necessary for us? Well, take your choice. The tortures occur. If they are unnecessary, then there is no God or a bad one. If there is a good God, then these tortures are necessary. For no even moderately good Being could possibly inflict or permit them if they weren't.

Either way, we're for it.

What do people mean when they say 'I am not afraid of God because I know He is good'? Have they never even been to a dentist?

Yet this is unendurable. And then one babbles – 'If

only I could bear it, or the worst of it, or any of it, instead of her.' But one can't tell how serious that bid is, for nothing is staked on it. If it suddenly became a real possibility, then, for the first time, we should discover how seriously we had meant it. But is it ever allowed?

It was allowed to One, we are told, and I find I can now believe again, that He has done vicariously whatever can be so done. He replies to our babble, 'You cannot and you dare not. I could and dared.'

Something quite unexpected has happened. It came this morning early. For various reasons, not in themselves at all mysterious, my heart was lighter than it had been for many weeks. For one thing, I suppose I am recovering physically from a good deal of mere exhaustion. And I'd had a very tiring but very healthy twelve hours the day before, and a sounder night's sleep; and after ten days of low-hung grey skies and motionless warm dampness, the sun was shining and there was a light breeze. And suddenly at the very moment when, so far, I mourned H least, I remembered her best. Indeed it was something (almost) better than memory; an instantaneous, unanswerable impression. To say it was like a meeting would be going too far. Yet there was that in it which tempts one to use those words. It was as if the lifting of the sorrow removed a barrier.

Why has no one told me these things? How easily I might have misjudged another man in the same situation? I might have said, 'He's got over it. He's forgotten his wife,' when the truth was, 'He remembers her better *because* he has partly got over it.'

Such was the fact. And I believe I can make sense out of it. You can't see anything properly while your eyes are blurred with tears. You can't, in most things, get what you want if you want it too desperately: anyway, you can't get the best out of it. 'Now! Let's have a real good talk' reduces everyone to silence, 'I *must* get a good sleep tonight' ushers in hours of wakefulness. Delicious drinks are wasted on a really ravenous thirst. Is it similarly the very intensity of the longing that draws the iron curtain, that makes us feel we are staring into a vacuum when we think about our dead? 'Them as asks' (at any rate 'as asks too importunately') don't get. Perhaps can't.

And so, perhaps, with God. I have gradually been coming to feel that the door is no longer shut and bolted. Was it my own frantic need that slammed it in my face? The time when there is nothing at all in your soul except a cry for help may be just the time when God can't give it: you are like the drowning man who can't be helped because he clutches and grabs. Perhaps your own reiterated cries deafen you to the voice you hoped to hear.

On the other hand, 'Knock and it shall be opened.' But does knocking mean hammering and kicking the door like a maniac? And there's also 'To him that hath shall be given.' After all, you must have a capacity to receive, or even omnipotence can't give. Perhaps your own passion temporarily destroys the capacity.

For all sorts of mistakes are possible when you are dealing with Him. Long ago, before we were married, H was haunted all one morning as she went about her work with the obscure sense of God (so to speak) 'at her elbow', demanding her attention. And of course, not being a perfected saint, she had the feeling that it would be a question, as it usually is, of some unrepented sin or tedious duty. At last she gave in – I know how one puts it off – and faced Him. But the message was, 'I want to *give* you something' and instantly she entered into joy.

I think I am beginning to understand why grief feels like suspense. It comes from the frustration of so many impulses that had become habitual. Thought after thought, feeling after feeling, action after action, had H for their object. Now their target is gone. I keep on through habit fitting an arrow to the string; then I remember and have to lay the bow down. So many roads lead thought to H. I set out on one of them. But now there's an impassable frontier-post across it. So many roads once; now so many *culs de sac*.

For a good wife contains so many persons in herself. What was H not to me? She was my daughter and my mother, my pupil and my teacher, my subject and my sovereign; and always, holding all these in solution, my trusty comrade, friend, shipmate, fellow-soldier. My mistress; but at the same time all that any man friend (and I have good ones) has ever been to me. Perhaps more. If we had never fallen in love we should have none the less been always together, and created a scandal. That's what I meant when I once praised her for her 'masculine virtues'. But she soon put a stop to that by asking how I'd like to be praised for my feminine ones. It was a good *riposte*, dear. Yet there was something of the Amazon, something of Penthesileia and Camilla. And you, as well as I, were glad it should be there. You were glad I should recognize it.

Solomon calls his bride Sister. Could a woman be a complete wife unless, for a moment, in one particular mood, a man felt almost inclined to call her Brother?

'It was too perfect to last,' so I am tempted to say of our marriage. But it can be meant in two ways. It may be grimly pessimistic – as if God no sooner saw two of His creatures happy than He stopped it ('None of that here!'). As if He were like the Hostess at the sherry party who separates two guests the moment they show signs of having got into a real conversation. But it could also mean 'This had reached its proper perfection. This had become what it had in it to be. Therefore of course it would not be prolonged.' As if God said, 'Good; you have mastered that exercise. I am very pleased with it. And now you are ready to go on to the next.' When you have learned to do quadratics and enjoy doing them you will not be set them much longer. The teacher moves you on.

For we did learn and achieve something. There is, hidden or flaunted, a sword between the sexes till an entire marriage reconciles them. It is arrogance in us to call frankness, fairness, and chivalry 'masculine' when we see them in a woman; it is arrogance in them, to describe a man's sensitiveness or tact or tenderness as 'feminine'. But also what poor, warped fragments of humanity most mere men and mere women must be to make the implications of that arrogance plausible. Marriage heals this. Jointly the two become fully human. 'In the image of God created He *them*.' Thus, by a paradox, this carnival of sexuality leads us out beyond our sexes.

And then one or other dies. And we think of this as love cut short; like a dance stopped in mid career or a flower with its head unluckily snapped off – something truncated and therefore, lacking its due shape. I wonder. If, as I can't help suspecting, the dead also feel the pains of separation (and this may be one of their purgatorial sufferings), then for both lovers, and for all pairs of lovers without exception, bereavement is a universal and integral part of our experience of love. It follows marriage as normally as marriage follows courtship or as autumn follows summer. It is not a truncation of the process but one of its phases; not the interruption of the dance, but the next figure. We are 'taken out of ourselves' by the loved one while she is here. Then comes the tragic figure of the dance in which we must learn to be still taken out of ourselves though the bodily presence is withdrawn, to love the very Her, and not fall back to loving our past, or our memory, or our sorrow, or our relief from sorrow, or our own love.

Looking back, I see that only a very little time ago I was greatly concerned about my memory of H and how false it might become. For some reason – the merciful good sense of God is the only one I can think of – I have stopped bothering about that. And the remarkable thing is that since I stopped bothering about it, she seems to meet me everywhere. *Meet* is far too strong a word. I don't mean anything remotely like an apparition or a voice. I don't mean even any strikingly emotional experience at any particular moment. Rather, a sort of unobtrusive but massive sense that she is, just as much as ever, a fact to be taken into account.

'To be taken into account' is perhaps an unfortunate way of putting it. It sounds as if she were rather a battle-axe. How can I put it better? Would 'momentously real' or 'obstinately real' do? It is as if the experience said to me 'You are, as it happens, extremely glad that H is still a fact. But remember she would be equally a fact whether you liked it or not. Your preferences have not been considered.'

How far have I got? Just as far, I think, as a widower of another sort who would stop, leaning on his spade, and say in answer to our inquiry, 'Thank 'ee. Musn't grumble. I do miss her something dreadful. But they say these things are sent to try us.' We have come to the same point; he with his spade, and I, who am not now much good at digging, with my own instrument. But of course one must take 'sent to try us' the right way. God has not been trying an experiment on my faith or love in order to find out their quality. He knew it already. It was I who didn't. In this trial He makes us occupy the dock, the witness box, and the bench all at once. He always knew that my temple was a house of cards. His only way of making me realize the fact was to knock it down.

Getting over it so soon? But the words are ambiguous. To say the patient is getting over it after an operation for appendicitis is one thing; after he's had his leg off it is quite another. After that operation either the wounded stump heals or the man dies. If it heals, the fierce, continuous pain will stop. Presently he'll get back his strength and be able to stump about on his wooden leg. He has 'got over it'. But he will probably have recurrent pains in the stump all his life, and perhaps pretty bad ones; and he will always be a one-legged man. There will be hardly any moment when he forgets it. Bathing, dressing, sitting down and getting up again, even lying in bed, will all be different. His whole way of life will be changed. All sorts of pleasures and activities that he once took for granted will have to be simply written off. Duties too. At present I am learning to get about on crutches. Perhaps I shall presently be given a wooden leg. But I shall never be a biped again.

Still, there's no denying that in some sense I 'feel better', and with that comes at once a sort of shame, and a feeling that one is under a sort of obligation to cherish and foment and prolong one's unhappiness. I've read about that in books, but I never dreamed I should feel it myself. I am sure H wouldn't approve of it. She'd tell me not to be a fool. So I'm pretty certain, would God. What is behind it?

Partly, no doubt, vanity. We want to prove to ourselves that we are lovers on the grand scale, tragic heroes; not just ordinary privates in the huge army of the bereaved, slogging along and making the best of a bad job. But that's not the whole of the explanation.

I think there is also a confusion. We don't really want grief, in its first agonies, to be prolonged: nobody could. But we want something else of which grief is a frequent symptom, and then we confuse the symptom with the thing itself. I wrote the other night that bereavement is not the truncation of married love but one of its regular phases – like the honeymoon. What we want is to live our marriage well and faithfully through that phase too. If it hurts (and it certainly will) we accept the pains as a necessary part of this phase. We don't want to escape them at the price of desertion or divorce. Killing the dead a second time. We were one flesh. Now that it has been cut in two, we don't want to pretend that it is whole and complete. We will be still married, still in love. Therefore we shall still ache. But we are not at all – if we understand ourselves – seeking the aches for their own sake. The less of them the better, so long as the marriage is preserved. And the more joy there can be in the marriage between dead and living, the better.

The better in every way. For, as I have discovered, passionate grief does not link us with the dead but cuts us off from them. This becomes clearer and clearer. It is just at those moments when I feel least sorrow – getting into my morning bath is usually one of them – that H rushes upon my mind in her full reality, her otherness. Not, as in my worst moments, all foreshortened and patheticized and solemnized by my miseries, but as she is in her own right. This is good and tonic.

I seem to remember – though I couldn't quote one at the moment – all sorts of ballads and folk-tales in which the dead tell us that our mourning does them some kind of wrong. They beg us to stop it. There may be far more depth in this than I thought. If so, our grandfathers' generation went very far astray. All that (sometimes lifelong) ritual of sorrow – visiting graves, keeping anniversaries, leaving the empty bedroom exactly as 'the departed' used to keep it, mentioning the dead either not at all or always in a special voice, or even (like Queen Victoria) having the dead man's clothes put out for dinner every evening – this was like mummification. It made the dead far more dead.

Or was that (unconsciously) its purpose? Something very primitive may be at work here. To keep the dead thoroughly dead, to make sure that they won't come sidling back among the living, is a main pre-occupation of the savage mind. At all costs make them 'stay put'. Certainly these rituals do in fact emphasize their deadness. Perhaps this result was not really so unwelcome, not always, as the ritualists believed.

But I've no business to judge them. All guesswork; I'd better keep my breath to cool my own porridge. For me at any rate the programme is plain. I will turn to her as often as possible in gladness. I will even salute her with a laugh. The less I mourn her the nearer I seem to her.

An admirable programme. Unfortunately it can't be carried out. Tonight all the hells of young grief have opened again; the mad words, the bitter resentment, the fluttering in the stomach, the nightmare unreality, the wallowed-in tears. For in grief nothing 'stays put'. One keeps on emerging from a phase, but it always recurs.

Round and round. Everything repeats. Am I going in circles, or dare I hope I am on a spiral?

But if a spiral, am I going up or down it?

How often – will it be for always? – how often will the vast emptiness astonish me like a complete novelty and make me say, 'I never realized my loss till this moment'? The same leg is cut off time after time. The first plunge of the knife into the flesh is felt again and again.

They say 'The coward dies many times'; so does the beloved. Didn't the eagle find a fresh liver to tear in Prometheus every time it dined?

FOUR

This is the fourth – and the last – empty MS book I can find in the house; at least nearly empty, for there are some pages of very ancient arithmetic at the end by J. I resolve to let this limit my jottings. I *will not* start buying books for the purpose. In so far as this record was a defence against total collapse, a safety-valve, it has done some good. The other end I had in view turns out to have been based on a misunderstanding. I thought I could describe a *state*; make a map of sorrow. Sorrow, however, turns out to be not a state but a process. It needs not a map but a history, and if I don't stop writing that history at some quite arbitrary point, there's no reason why I should ever stop. There is something new to be chronicled every day. Grief is like a long valley, a winding valley where any bend may reveal a totally new landscape. As I've already noted, not every bend does. Sometimes the surprise is the opposite one; you are presented with exactly the same sort of country you thought you had left behind miles ago. That is when you wonder whether the valley isn't a circular trench. But it isn't. There are partial recurrences, but the sequence doesn't repeat.

Here, for instance, is a new phase, a new loss. I do all the walking I can, for I'd be a fool to go to bed not tired. Today I have been revisiting old haunts, taking one of the long rambles that made me so happy in my bachelor days. And this time the face of nature was not emptied of its beauty and the world didn't look (as I complained some days ago) like a mean street. On the contrary, every horizon, every stile or clump of trees, summoned me into a past kind of happiness, my pre-H happiness. But the invitation seemed to me horrible. The happiness into which it invited me was insipid. I find that I don't want to go back again and be happy in *that* way. It frightens me to think that a mere going back should even be possible. For this fate would seem to me the worst of all; to reach a state in which my years of love and marriage should appear in retrospect a charming episode – like a holiday – that had briefly interrupted my interminable life and returned me to normal, unchanged. And then it would come to seem unreal – something so foreign to the usual texture of my history that I could almost believe it had happened to someone else. Thus H would die to me a second time; a worse bereavement than the first. Anything but that.

Did you ever know, dear, how much you took away with you when you left? You have stripped me even of my past, even of the things we never shared. I was wrong to say the stump was recovering from the pain of the amputation. I was deceived because it has so many ways to hurt me that I discover them only one by one.

Still, there are the two enormous gains – I know myself too well now to call them 'lasting'. Turned to God, my mind no longer meets that locked door; turned to H, it no longer meets that vacuum – nor all that fuss about my mental image of her. My jottings show something of the process, but not so much as I'd hoped. Perhaps both changes were really not observable. There was no sudden, striking, and emotional transition. Like the warming of a room or the coming of daylight. When you first notice them they have already been going on for some time.

The notes have been about myself, and about H, and about God. In that order. The order and the proportions exactly what they ought not to have been. And I see that I have nowhere fallen into that mode of thinking about either which we call praising them. Yet that would have been best for me. Praise is the mode of love which always has some element of joy in it. Praise in due order; of Him as the giver, of her as the gift. Don't we in praise somehow enjoy what we praise, however far we are from it? I must do more of this. I have lost the fruition I once had of H. And I am far, far away in the valley of my unlikeness, from the fruition which, if His mercies are infinite, I may some time have of God. But by praising I can still, in some degree, enjoy her, and already, in some degree, enjoy Him. Better than nothing.

But perhaps I lack the gift. I see I've described H as being like a sword. That's true as far as it goes. But utterly inadequate by itself, and misleading. I ought to have balanced it. I ought to have said 'But also like a garden. Like a nest of gardens, wall within wall, hedge within hedge, more secret, more full of fragrant and fertile life, the further you entered.'

And then, of her, and of every created thing I praise, I should say 'In some way, in its unique way, like Him who made it'.

Thus up from the garden to the Gardener, from the sword to the Smith. To the life-giving Life and the Beauty that makes beautiful.

'She is in God's hand.' That gains a new energy when I think of her as a sword. Perhaps the earthly life I shared with her was only part of the tempering. Now perhaps He grasps the hilt; weighs the new weapon; makes lightnings with it in the air. 'A right Jerusalem blade.'

One moment last night can be described in similes; otherwise it won't go into language at all. Imagine a man in total darkness. He thinks he is in a cellar or dungeon. Then there comes a sound. He thinks it might be a sound from far off – waves or wind blown trees or cattle half a mile away. And if so, it proves he's not in a cellar, but free, in the open air. Or it may be a much smaller sound close at hand – a chuckle of laughter. And if so, there is a friend just beside him in the dark. Either way, a good, good sound. I'm not mad enough to take such an experience as evidence for anything. It is simply the leaping into imaginative activity of an idea which I would always have theoretically admitted – the idea that I, or any mortal at any time, may be utterly mistaken as to the situation he is really in.

Five senses; an incurably abstract intellect; a haphazardly selective memory; a set of preconceptions and assumptions so numerous that I can never examine more than a minority of them all. How much of total reality can such an apparatus let through?

I will not, if I can help it, shin up either the feathery or the prickly tree. Two widely different convictions press more and more on my mind. One is that the Eternal Vet is even more inexorable and the possible operations even more painful than our severest imaginings can forbode. But the other, that 'all shall be well, and all shall be well, and all manner of thing shall be well'.

It doesn't matter that all the photographs of H are bad. It doesn't matter – not much – if my memory of her is imperfect. Images, whether on paper or in the mind, are not important for themselves. Merely links. Take a parallel from an infinitely higher sphere. Tomorrow morning a priest will give me a little round, thin, cold, tasteless wafer. Is it a disadvantage – is it not in some ways an advantage – that it can't pretend the least *resemblance* to that with which it unites me?

I need Christ, not something that resembles Him. I want H, not something that is like her. A really good photograph might become in the end a snare, a horror, and an obstacle.

Images, I must suppose, have their use or they would not have been so popular. (It makes little difference whether they are pictures and statues outside the mind or imaginative constructions within it.) To me, however, their danger is more obvious. Images of the Holy easily become holy images – sacrosanct. My idea of God is not a divine idea. It has to be shattered time after time. He shatters it Himself. He is the great iconoclast. Could we not almost say that this shattering is one of the marks of His presence? The Incarnation is the supreme example; it leaves all previous ideas of the Messiah in ruins. And most are 'offended' by the iconoclasm; and blessed are those who are not. But the same thing happens in our private prayers.

All reality is iconoclastic. The earthly beloved, even in this life, incessantly triumphs over your mere idea of her. And you want her to; you want her with all her resistances, all her faults, all her unexpectedness. That is, in her foursquare and independent reality. And this, not any image or memory, is what we are to love still, after she is dead.

But 'this' is not now imaginable. In that respect H and all the dead are like God. In that respect loving her has become, in its measure, like loving Him. In both cases I must stretch out the arms and hands of love – its eyes cannot here be used – to the reality, through – across – all the changeful phantasmagoria of my thoughts, passions, and imaginings. I mustn't sit down content with the phantasmagoria itself and worship that for Him, or love that for her.

Not my idea of God, but God. Not my idea of H, but H. Yes, and also not my idea of my neighbour, but my neighbour. For don't we often make this mistake as regards people who are still alive – who are with us in the same room? Talking and acting not to the man himself but to the picture – almost the *précis* – we've made of him in our own minds? And he has to depart from it pretty widely before we even notice the fact. In real life – that's one way it differs from novels – his words and acts are, if we observe closely, hardly ever quite 'in character', that is, in what we call his character. There's always a card in his hand we didn't know about.

My reason for assuming that I do this to other people is the fact that so often I find them obviously doing it to me. We all think we've got one another taped.

And all this time I may, once more, be building with cards. And if I am He will once more knock the building flat. He will knock it down as often as proves necessary.

Unless I have to be finally given up as hopeless, and left building pasteboard palaces in Hell forever; 'free among the dead'.

Am I, for instance, just sidling back to God because I know that if there's any road to H, it runs through Him? But then of course I know perfectly well that He can't be used as a road. If you're approaching Him not as the goal but as a road, not as the end but as a means, you're not really approaching Him at all. That's what was really wrong with all those popular pictures of happy re-unions 'on the further shore'; not the simple-minded and very earthly images, but the fact that they make an End of what we can get only as a by-product of the true End.

Lord, are these your real terms? Can I meet H again only if I learn to love you so much that I don't care whether I meet her or not? Consider, Lord, how it looks to us. What would anyone think of me if I said to the boys, 'No toffee now. But when you've grown up and don't really want toffee you shall have as much of it as you choose'?

If I knew that to be eternally divided from H and eternally forgotten by her would add a greater joy and splendour to her being, of course I'd say 'Fire ahead'. Just as if, on earth, I could have cured her cancer by never seeing her again, I'd have arranged never to see her again. I'd have had to. Any decent person would. But that's quite different. That's not the situation I'm in.

When I lay these questions before God I get no answer. But a rather special sort of 'No answer'. It is not the locked door. It is more like a silent, certainly not uncompassionate, gaze. As though He shook His head not in refusal but waiving the question. Like, 'Peace, child; you don't understand.'

Can a mortal ask questions which God finds unanswerable? Quite easily, I should think. All nonsense questions are unanswerable. How many hours are there in a mile? Is yellow square or round? Probably half the questions we ask – half our great theological and metaphysical problems – are like that.

And now that I come to think of it, there's no practical problem before me at all. I know the two great commandments, and I'd better get on with them. Indeed, H's death has ended the practical problem. While she was alive I could, in practice, have put her before God; that is, could have done what she wanted instead of what He wanted; if there'd been a conflict. What's left is not a problem about anything I could *do*. It's all about weights of feelings and motives and that sort of thing. It's a problem I'm setting myself. I don't believe God set it me at all.

The fruition of God. Re-union with the dead. These can't figure in my thinking except as counters. Blank cheques. My idea – if you can call it an idea – of the first is a huge, risky extrapolation from a very few and short experiences here on earth. Probably not such valuable experiences as I think. Perhaps even of less value than others that I take no account of. My idea of the second is also an extrapolation. The reality of either – the cashing of either cheque – would probably blow all one's ideas about both (how much more one's ideas about their relations to each other) into smithereens.

The mystical union on the one hand. The resurrection of the body, on the other. I can't reach the ghost of an image, a formula, or even a feeling, that combines them. But the reality, we are given to understand, does. Reality the iconoclast once more. Heaven will solve our problems, but not, I think, by showing us subtle reconciliations between all our apparently contradictory notions. The notions will all be knocked from under our feet. We shall see that there never was any problem.

And, more than once, that impression which I can't describe except by saying that it's like the sound of a chuckle in the darkness. The sense that some shattering and disarming simplicity is the real answer.

It is often thought that the dead see us. And we assume, whether reasonably or not, that if they see us at all they see us more clearly than before. Does H now see exactly how much froth or tinsel there was in what she called, and I call, my love? So be it. Look your hardest, dear. I wouldn't hide if I could. We didn't idealize each other. We tried to keep no secrets. You knew most of the rotten places in me already. If you now see anything worse, I can take it. So can you. Rebuke, explain, mock, forgive. For this is one of the miracles of love; it gives – to both, but perhaps especially to the woman – a power of seeing through its own enchantments and yet not being disenchanted.

To see, in some measure, like God. His love and His knowledge are not distinct from one another, nor from Him. We could almost say He sees because He loves, and therefore loves although He sees.

Sometimes, Lord, one is tempted to say that if you wanted us to behave like the lilies of the field you might have given us an organization more like theirs. But that, I suppose, is just your grand experiment. Or no; not an experiment, for you have no need to find things out. Rather your grand enterprise. To make an organism which is also a spirit; to make that terrible oxymoron, a 'spiritual animal'. To take a poor primate, a beast with nerve-endings all over it, a creature with a stomach that wants to be filled, a breeding animal that wants its mate, and say, 'Now get on with it. Become a god.'

I said, several notebooks ago, that even if I got what seemed like an assurance of H's presence, I wouldn't believe it. Easier said than done. Even now, though, I won't treat anything of that sort as evidence. It's the *quality* of last night's experience – not what it proves but what it was – that makes it worth putting down. It was quite incredibly unemotional. Just the impression of her *mind* momentarily facing my own. Mind, not 'soul' as we tend to think of soul. Certainly the reverse of what is called 'soulful'. Not at all like a rapturous re-union of lovers. Much more like getting a telephone call or a wire from her about some practical arrangement. Not that there was any 'message' – just intelligence and attention. No sense of joy or sorrow. No love even, in our ordinary sense. No un-love. I had never in any mood imagined the dead as being so – well, so business-like. Yet there was an extreme and cheerful intimacy. An intimacy that had not passed through the senses or the emotions at all.

If this was a throw-up from my unconscious, then my unconscious must be a far more interesting region than the depth psychologists have led me to expect. For one thing, it is apparently much less primitive than my consciousness.

Wherever it came from, it has made a sort of spring cleaning in my mind. The dead could be like that; sheer intellects. A Greek philosopher wouldn't have been surprised at an experience like mine. He would have expected that if anything of us remained after death it would be just that. Up to now this always seemed to me a most arid and chilling idea. The absence of emotion repelled me. But in this contact (whether real or apparent) it didn't do anything of the sort. One didn't need emotion. The intimacy was complete – sharply bracing and restorative too – without it. Can that intimacy be love itself – always in this life attended with emotion, not because it is itself an emotion, or needs an attendant emotion, but because our animal souls, our nervous systems, our imaginations, have to respond to it in that way? If so, how many preconceptions I must scrap! A society, a communion, of pure intelligence would not be cold, drab and comfortless. On the other hand it wouldn't be very like what people usually mean when they use such words as 'spiritual', or 'mystical', or 'holy'. It would, if I have had a glimpse, be – well, I'm almost scared at the adjectives I'd have to use. Brisk? cheerful? keen? alert? intense? wide-awake? Above all, solid. Utterly reliable. Firm. There is no nonsense about the dead.

When I say 'intellect' I include will. Attention is an act of will. Intelligence in action is will *par excellence*. What seemed to meet me was full of resolution.

Once very near the end I said, 'If you can – if it is allowed – come to me when I too am on my death bed.' 'Allowed!' she said. 'Heaven would have a job to hold me; and as for Hell, I'd break it into bits.' She knew she was speaking a kind of mythological language, with even an element of comedy in it. There was a twinkle as well as a tear in her eye. But there was no myth and no joke about the will, deeper than any feeling, that flashed through her.

But I mustn't, because I have come to misunderstand a little less completely what a pure intelligence might be, lean over too far. There is also, whatever it means, the resurrection of the body. We cannot understand. The best is perhaps what we understand least.

Didn't people dispute once whether the final vision of God was more an act of intelligence or of love? That is probably another of the nonsense questions.

How wicked it would be, if we could, to call the dead back! She said not to me but to the chaplain, 'I am at peace with God.' She smiled, but not at me. *Poi si tornò all' eterna fontana.*

II

READERS ON
A Grief Observed

Hilary Mantel

'No one ever told me that grief felt so like fear.' With his first line, C. S. Lewis reacquaints his reader with the physiology of mourning; he brings into each mouth the common taste of private and personal loss. 'I know something of this,' you think. Even if you have not experienced a 'front line' bereavement, like the loss of partner, parent or child, you have certainly lost something you value: a marriage or a job, an internal organ or some aspect of mind or body that defines who you are. Perhaps you have just lost yourself on your way through life, lost your chances or your reputation or your integrity, or chosen to lose bad memories by pushing them into a personal and portable tomb. Perhaps you have merely wasted time, and seethe with frustration because you can't recall it. The pattern of all losses mirrors the pattern of the gravest losses. Disbelief is followed by numbness, numbness by distraction, despair, exhaustion. Your former life still seems to exist somewhere, but you can't get back to it; there is a glimpse in dreams of those peacock lawns and fountains, but you're fenced out, and each morning you wake up to the loss over again. Grief is like fear in the way it gnaws the gut. Your mind is on a short tether, turning round and round. You fear to focus on your grief but cannot concentrate on anything else. You look with incredulity at those going about their ordinary lives. There is a gulf between you and them, as if you had been stranded on an island for lepers; and indeed C. S. Lewis wonders whether a grieving person should be put in isolation like a leper, to avoid the awkwardness of encounters with the unbereaved, who don't know what to say and, though they feel good will, exhibit something like shame.

C. S. Lewis, now most celebrated as a writer for children, was also one of the great Christian thinkers of the last century. His memoir *Surprised by Joy*, written before his marriage, is an absorbing account of childhood and a luminous description of his conversion experience. In 1956 he was lured out of his donnish bachelor state by Joy Davidman, an American poet. By his marriage he became stepfather to two boys. His life flowered. But four years later Joy died of cancer. Born in 1898, educated at a public school, an officer in the Great War, an intellectual, a man who (by his own account) feared the collective and feared the feminine, Lewis found himself plunged into an experience against which intellect could not defend him, a process that is as common as the air we breathe, a process that involves a feminine dissolution into 'pathos and tears'. In his memoir he recalls the death of his mother when he was a small boy. 'Grief was overwhelmed by terror' at the sight of her corpse, and he was not helped to mourn, his natural grief subsumed into the violent reactions of adults. The work of mourning, if not performed when it is due, seems to be stored up for us, often for many years. It compounds and complicates our later griefs. The loss of his wife plunged Lewis into the crisis of faith this book explores.

Why had she been taken away, when his marriage had made him a more complete human being? As a theologian he would come to credit God with some subtlety, but as a man he must have felt he had been thrown back into the classroom at his prep school, with its routinely hellish regime of arbitrary beatings. He soon saw that mourning kicks away the props we rely on. It confiscates our cognitive assets and undermines our rationality. It frequently undermines any religious faith we may have, and did so in this case. In his 1940 book *The Problem of Pain*, Lewis tackled what Muriel Spark, in the title of a novel, called *The Only Problem*: if God is good, why does he permit the innocent to suffer? Lewis had worked over the ground in theory. After his wife's death he had to do the work again, this time in raw dismay: dismay not only at the terrible event itself, but at his reaction to it. Unless his faith in the afterlife is childish and literal, the pain of loss is often intensified for a believer, because he feels angry with his god and feels shame and guilt about that anger; this being so, you wonder how the idea began, that religion is a consolation. It is not that Lewis ceases to believe in God. It is that he is horrified at what he suspects about God's nature. How can one not rebel against such perceived cruelty? Conventional consolations are offered to him, and seem to miss the point. 'You tell me "she goes on". But my heart and body are crying out, come back, come back.' The Christian finds himself at heart a pagan, wishing to descend, like Orpheus, into the underworld, to lead the lost person back into the light.

Gradually the shape of loss emerges, but it is complex and ever-changing. Grief gives the whole of life 'a permanently provisional feeling'. Sorrow is 'a long valley, a winding valley where any bend may reveal a totally new landscape'. The dead person recedes, losing selfhood, losing integrity, becoming an artefact of memory. The process creates panic and guilt; are we remembering properly? Are we remembering enough? A year passes, but each day the loss strikes us as an absolute novelty. When Lewis wrote *A Grief Observed*, he did not objectify his grief in the language of psychology, but alternated between the terms available to, on the one hand, the spiritual seeker, and on the other hand the stricken child. Nowadays, most of us have a humanist vocabulary at our command, but sometimes it seems no help at all. In 1969, in her influential book *On Death and Dying*, Elisabeth Kübler-Ross defined five stages of grief: deni-

al, anger, bargaining, depression, acceptance. The model
she created is apt to be misunderstood as a linear model,
and can be used, by inept counsellors or half-informed
friends, as a way of bullying the bereaved. What, are
you stuck? Going round and round instead of forwards?
Still mired in 'depression', two years on? Perhaps you
need a psychiatrist. Mechanical efficacy is attributed to
the passage of time, but those in mourning know how
time doubles and deceives. And though, in this country, self-restraint is said to have vanished with Princess
Diana, sometimes it seems the world still expects the
bereaved person to 'move on' briskly, and meanwhile
behave in a way that does not embarrass the rest of us.
In *The Year of Magical Thinking*, Joan Didion's memoir of her husband's death, she writes of our dread of
self-pity: Lewis too experienced this. We would rather
be harsh to ourselves, harsher than a stranger would be,
than be accused of 'wallowing', of 'dwelling on it'.

But where else can the bereft person dwell, except in
his grief? He is like a vagrant, carrying with him the
package of tribulation that is all he owns. As Lewis says,
'So many roads once; now so many *culs de sac*.' It is hard
to spot signs of recovery, hard to evaluate them. Lewis
asks, 'Am I going in circles, or dare I hope I am on a spiral?' The first acute agony cannot last, but the sufferer
dreads what will replace it. For Lewis, a lightening of the
heart produces, paradoxically, a more vivid impression

of his dead wife than he could conjure when he was in a pit of despair. Recovery can seem like a betrayal. Passionately, you desire a way back to the lost object, but the only possible road, the road to life, leads away.

Lewis's book is a lucid description of an obscure, muddled process, a process almost universal, one with no logic and no timetable. It is an honest attempt to write about aspects of the human and the divine which, he fears, 'won't go into language at all'. At the heart of the enterprise is his quarrel with God, and in the end God wins, first philosophically, then emotionally. But there is a puzzle as to how to categorise the book: where should it be shelved? Lewis's reputation being what it is, it would be natural to place it under 'Religion'. But many of the people who need it would not find it there because, like Lewis, they are angrily running away from God, hurtling to abandon a being who seems to have abandoned them. It is more a book about doubt than about faith; it does not warn, exhort or seek to convince. Anger finds a voice in this book, more anger than the faithful are usually able to acknowledge. But it doesn't belong in the 'self-help' section either: it has no bullet points, suggests no programme, offers no cheering anecdotes. What it does do is to make the reader live more consciously. Testimony from a sensitive and eloquent witness, it should be placed on a shelf that doesn't exist, in the section called 'The Human Condition'. It offers an interrogation of experience and a glimmer of hard-won hope. It allows one bewildered mind to reach out to another. Death is no barrier to that.

Jessica Martin

Towards the close of *A Grief Observed* C. S. Lewis writes, 'All reality is iconoclastic.' It's such a flatly uncompromising statement that it sounds like an aphorism, but it's more experimental than that. Driven over and over between describing the sensations of anguish, and positing (out of an 'incurably abstract intellect') hypotheses about the intentions of God to his suffering creatures, Lewis finds a temporary point of imaginative and intellectual rest. It is a kind of holy of holies, a room scoured of the heart's images, impervious to the mind's constructions. These are to be resisted and destroyed. Take your hammer and knock them down! The place is emptied to allow the possibility of a presence he has not himself made. In the few pages that follow he describes, for the first time, patchily, a visiting consolation.

Rhetorically, this is tremendously effective. After reading vivid accounts of this, or that, state of mind in bereavement; of this or that wounded attempt to ease an unappeasable pain, why should this final sense of beloved presence not be another construction of the grieving mind? Is this any more a place to stop than any other respite on the cycle? But if we know that Lewis has taken a hammer to his idols we also know that this consoling presence is real.

Lewis's dilemma, as a writer, was of one whose skill to move tended to occlude, for himself, the very experience he sought to express. This time, this book, Lewis is deeply impatient of his professional capacity to stand in his own light – much more impatient than was ever the case when he wrote only about God. He knows this, of course – contrasting more than once the emotional urgency of his present wrestlings with neater past opinings. The idea of the empty room, the image-free, unmanipulable reality impervious to rhetoric, seems a beguiling solution, an open place finally absent of the endlessly talking self.

Except that it isn't. Not quite. Lewis is a maker, a good one. Just because he sees ways to convey resistant experience that will translate it into partial intelligibility, this says nothing either way about the authenticity of the experience itself. He must have known that – if not when he was writing the notes which became *A Grief Observed* then at any rate when he was shaping it for publication. Were silence his cure for illusion he would not be considering a readership.

Yet even empty rooms must have dimensions: walls, a roof, a quality of light, space for a window. Above all, rooms are for living in; spaces for someone else to alight or even abide.

And so he resigns himself to imagining a steady something out of the unsteady materials of loss. His method is stoical, documentary. His only defence is the swagger of an apparent dispassion, a kind of Spartan-boy approach to pain that has a touch of machismo about it, but is as temporary an attitude as any of the others. Below every mood lies a more genuinely dispassionate regard for the loadbearing capacities of literary effect. He is harnessing grief into work. At one point he compares himself to 'a widower of another sort who would stop, leaning on his spade, and say . . . "Musn't grumble"'. Lewis cannot dig but he is ashamed to beg: he has his own instrument of work, and with it has 'come to the same point' as his fellow widower with his spade. The grief he is trying to build with is not only his own; he is seeing whether, even in this extremity, he can manage to be everyman.

He doesn't – thank goodness – find this easy. There are things he can't do any more, some everyman *personae* he's not going to attempt. Sometimes the gulf he bridges between himself and others' experience has to traverse a fastidious refusal to join the company and emotional habits of the bereaved. The story he tells of his instinctive horror at the man who calls tending her grave 'going to visit Mum' is of that kind. Any parish priest will know how many grieving children, siblings, wives, husbands, partners will invest in a tiny square of ground the lost personality with which, half guiltily, they converse as they change the flowers in the vase or weed the ground around the bulbs. What Lewis concludes from this is that the physical otherness of a grave at least saves the mourner from mistaking it for a lost reality. I think he is probably wrong about that.

Lewis is not by temperament an analyst (when he argues, he almost always cheats) and especially not here. His picture of himself as unflinchingly analytical is part of the whole Spartan-boy attitude; like his friend Dorothy Sayers he always had a weakness for grandstanding. Here his subject is emotion, and he is scrupulous; propositional building blocks are barely of interest except as they support the structures of grief. His thought experience is a 'spiral' (his word) following agony round to a place much like the last – 'Feelings, and feelings, and feelings. Let me try thinking instead.' The book moves in fiercely controlled oscillations; hardly any of its theoretical constructs are meant to last for more than a moment and even those that echo some version of theological orthodoxy – and here he tends to favour those on the bleaker side of doctrinal variation – are formally destroyed at intervals: 'some shattering and disarming simplicity is the real answer'.

The stabler conclusion the book builds is experiential: 'not what it proves but what it was', writes Lewis. Analogy and metaphor rely on pointing out that something *is not* altogether like the something else with which it is compared, and careful use of both protects him from confining or limiting the experience he is leaning on – like the expanses of white space that go with the journal form, pent with the influence of undescribed living. Truth is instead to be found in minute shifts of atmosphere. By the time we close the book his empty space has become filled with light, inhabited with a clear conversing presence who has been there a while, it is hard to say for how long. 'Like the warming of a room or the coming of daylight,' he writes. 'When you first notice them they have already been going on for some time.'

Jenna Bailey

Seven years ago my older sister Kate called in the middle of the night to tell me that 'the worst thing ever has happened'. She was right: our baby sister Emma had been killed in a car accident at the age of twenty-three. The driver of a Mercedes Sprinter van had fallen asleep on the M4 and collided with the car nearest him, causing his van to turn on its side, jump the central reservation into incoming traffic and race straight into Emma's vehicle, killing her instantly.

At night I am tormented by her death. I have a recurring dream, that in no way reflects the life we had together, in which Emma doesn't love me any more and doesn't want to be near me. I chase her and beg her to love me again. I plead with her. I feel desperate for the love she once gave me. Though these dreams break my heart, more painful are the moments between sleep and waking when I am overcome by the realisation that she is dead. In these sleepy moments I am not remembering her death, I am relearning it. For nights on end, I relive the horror of it. I feel the agony of this loss as acutely as I did on the day of her death and I awake feeling lost, angry and devastated.

For me these nightly occurrences are evidence of how, seven years on, my sister's death remains incomprehensible to me. Emma and I were best friends, twins born three years apart. We needed to be near each other and to share in each other's every day. We laughed constantly and loved each other tremendously. Having both moved away from our home in Canada to the UK, together we were sharing an exciting journey with Emma starting her career as an actress in London and my first book being released just months prior to her accident. That all of this could be taken away from us in one foolish, careless moment was inconceivable. The greatest difficulty for me lay in the fact that Emma and I were a package deal. To know me was to know her. We thought we were inseparable and yet here I was, suddenly so alone. I did not know how I could live when she was a half of me. How could I *exist* without Emma?

For months it was a struggle just to survive. Thinking, talking, eating, even breathing felt like a challenge, with grief overwhelming me physically and emotionally. At night I wept uncontrollably and prayed that I would die in my sleep, that I would not have to continue living in a world without Emma. Nothing could have prepared me for the enormity of this loss. In my desperation, like many bereaved people, I began to read about death and grief to help me understand what I was experiencing. It was through this process that I first read

A Grief Observed. Rereading C. S. Lewis's work now, with some distance from Emma's death, my instinct is to put the book away; I am almost fearful of his ability to convey his experience of grief so profoundly. I resist being reminded of how painful and consuming it can be. Yet, when I first encountered Lewis's writing, just three months after Emma's death, the opposite was true. I felt relieved to find a text that so clearly expressed so many aspects of the grief that I was experiencing. I, too, had a similar list of seemingly unanswerable questions, felt an 'invisible blanket' between myself and the world and was discovering that, as a bereaved person, I was a source of discomfort to many people around me.

What impacted me the most was Lewis's description of how grief involved the frustration of so many habitual thoughts, feelings and actions that had his wife as their object. After her death he continued to set out on the roads that led him to Joy but, in her absence, found that they were now *culs de sac.* Lewis's words perfectly articulated for me the suspended state in which I felt trapped. After a lifetime spent growing, sharing and being with Emma, I was left in a torturous limbo constantly looking for her, waiting for her, expecting her. I felt uncomfortable and unable to settle. I knew that she was not coming, that I would never hear her infectious laughter again, that I would never see her again, yet I couldn't help but look for her – that tendency was ingrained in my life, embedded in my being.

Just as Emma's presence had filled my life so fully, her absence stripped so much away. Not only did I lose my sister and best friend, so much of me died that day. I simply no longer knew how to *be*, without her. With time I realised that to survive I needed to alter my daily life and way of thinking dramatically and accept that the life I had and the person I was when Emma was alive no longer existed. The long, ongoing process of recovering from such a devastating loss has involved both learning to live without her and learning to become a new me. It has been a matter of relearning how to exist, rediscovering ways of finding happiness, and creating different habits, pathways and connections. Since I have had the strength to open these new doors, I have been surprised by the richness in life that is still available to me. With the unwavering support of countless friends and family, I have freed myself from the intolerable stasis that followed Emma's death and I once again have a remarkably happy life, which I know would make my sister so relieved and proud. Fundamental to this journey has been the acceptance that, while Emma's death has forever shaped me, it must be her life that influences me more. Hers was truly a joyful existence and I refuse to live without celebrating the happiness, hilarity, and selfless love she gave me. In this respect it is once again the words of C. S. Lewis that ring true when I think about how I will continue to live without her: 'I will turn to her as often as possible in gladness. I will even salute her with a laugh. The less I mourn her the nearer I seem to her.'

Rowan Williams

Long before Freud analysed 'Mourning and Melancholia', St Augustine was writing in his *Confessions* about the ambivalence of mourning. He describes his reaction to the death of a friend when both of them were around the age of twenty: the way in which all the places where they had spent time together became hateful because of the friend's absence; how the savour of resentment and self-pity became a dangerously comforting, warming, addictive taste; how he longed to get away from the places that reminded him of loss yet recognised that his own mind and body were the place where the loss was most felt and which could not be left or ignored. And in the middle of this extraordinary analysis comes an unforgettable phrase exclaiming at the *dementia* that 'doesn't know how to love human beings humanly'. The passionately loved friend, says Augustine, was more real and compelling than any abstract God (and he is candid about the feebleness of the view of God that he then held); but this vividness also conceals a very uncomfortable fact. The friend is vivid and lovable just because his existence is so bound up in his own fantasies and self-images. Now that he's dead, he 'lives in me';

but only as my possession, my source of consolation. What's left of him is the complicated bundle of self-regarding emotion I invested in him. No wonder he is more interesting than God: my deepest problem is always that I find myself more interesting than God.

Readers of C. S. Lewis's searing reflections will recognise the echoes immediately (Lewis will certainly have read Augustine's text, though he is not, I think, at any point consciously referring to it): the painful jolt of recognising the absence of a loved one in a particular place where you've shared happiness, the awful false consolation of self-pity, the 'one place I can't avoid' which is my own body, the threat of a dissolution of a real person into the doll/idol/fetish of my own needs and fancies – the pornography of grief, we might say. These two remarkable Christian self-analysts feel the same grain as they run their hands down the wood; and it has everything to do with the recognition of how difficult it is to believe not so much in God as in anything that isn't me.

Lewis writes about the 'the rough, sharp, cleansing tang of her otherness': her *otherness*. When someone is alive, they can always challenge and upset your myths about them, unless you are well on the way to solipsism and obsession. When they are dead, they are at your mercy. And whether or not you have a faith of any kind, it seems that you're faced with the terrible paradox that for them to be in some sense 'real', as real as they were for you in life, you have to prevent them becoming all in all to you – because this is to dehumanise them. You have to think what it means to love human beings humanly, for what they are, not what they aren't. They aren't God and they aren't you. They aren't the total meaning of your life and they aren't there just to be the total meaning of your life. They are other. And Lewis seems to suggest that one thing you will learn in bereavement is how far you have loved someone's difference, the tang of otherness.

This is a tough and not instantly consoling wisdom. Lewis's unsentimental approach might shock some believers and unbelievers too: whatever lies beyond death can't be a restoration of where we've been; it has to be something that pushes us into another level of growth. Hence Lewis's dismissive attitude to any simple talk about 'reunion' with loved ones in heaven, if that means a cosy reinstatement of the relation that has been. If you do believe in 'heaven', it's a transformation of every imaginable relationship (including relationship with God); if you don't, you still have to let go of being defined just by a relationship that *can no longer exist* – or, to put it rather starkly, can no longer defend itself against your ego and its fancies.

But Lewis is writing, uncompromisingly, as a believer; and to read this book adequately we have to notice what he says he has discovered about God. One of these things is said with a good deal of wry and bitter recognition. God *feels* like a sadist in moments of such acute pain (and pain because of the pain of others); but if he is, how can he at the same time be genuinely a creator, a power that overflows in the invention of things that give delight? Lewis – with a characteristic acidity about academic colleagues – turns to an academic colleague to illustrate the point. He has been sitting at dinner with a man describing his experiments in vivisection (something Lewis deeply loathed); and it is beyond imagining that someone like that could 'invent or create or govern anything'. '*He* make a universe? He couldn't make a joke, or a bow, or an apology, or a friend' (a sequence that tells you more about Lewis than many volumes of analysis). We can't dissolve the strangeness of all this by just another mythical projection, God as cosmic vivisector.

But the implication is also that God *cannot but* continuously shatter your images of him. And given what has been said about how it is only the living being that overturns our projections, that maintains the tang of otherness, it is the shifting, painfully expanding character of our thought about God that best shows what it means to call him 'living'. If our experience is littered with broken images of God – and deep pain and grief will certainly do this – then we are left either with no believable God at all or with a God whose otherness becomes daily more resistant and powerful; and alive.

Lewis ends with a picture drawn from Dante – the beloved turns away towards 'the eternal light'; 'She smiled, but not at me.' If the anguish of loss can be honestly lived in (not 'through'), it must be with a clear recognition of the impossibility of possessing or absorbing anyone we love. And for the believer, the deepest ground of such a recognition is that they are life-givingly connected with God before and after they are 'ours'. That there may be reality and joy which do not depend on my personal joy and truthfulness here and now is a hard doctrine. But if our love is more than self-serving, this is what we are asked to learn. And this is one of the things that Lewis, in this unsparing book, hopes to teach.

Kate Saunders

There is no consolation here, and no attempt to console. *A Grief Observed* is great because it articulates the roaring despair of bereavement from the eye of the storm. Amidst all the horror of losing his wife, Lewis the scholar couldn't help making scientific notes about the strange suburb of hell in which he found himself. And Lewis the Christian, who had assumed that he believed in a God who loved him, was not afraid to ask – what kind of loving God would do a thing like *this*?

The death of your best beloved hits you like a wrecker's ball. It's not that you stop believing in God, but that he has suddenly turned into a terrifying bastard – and an absent bastard at that. Just when you need him most he goes AWOL and stops answering the phone. Never have you cried into such a bottomless void. 'What chokes every prayer and every hope', as Lewis writes, 'is the memory of all the prayers H and I offered and all the false hopes we had.'

The last prayer I ever said was for my darling son Felix – as all my prayers had been, since before he was born. My Felix was a beautiful, talented, kind, funny boy of nineteen. From the start of 2012 he had been suffering agonies of clinical depression, but on that night in July I was full of hope (stupid hope, as it turns out; part of you blushes at the memory afterwards, as if you'd asked your bankrupt father for a pony). We'd had such a nice day, Felix was in such good spirits. We'd spent a pleasant evening laughing at *Family Guy*.

After I went to bed that night, Felix looked into my bedroom; he said it was to tell me something funny but it was really to say a loving goodbye. In the early hours of the next morning, my beautiful son killed himself.

I had begged God to bless my boy, and this was the answer I got. It was like a bank collapsing. I'd invested thousands of prayers in my darling boy over the years, assuming I was storing up points of some kind, but just when I needed to cash in my savings, the currency turned out to be utterly worthless. I'll quote Lewis again, since he expresses the feeling perfectly: 'A door slammed in your face, and a sound of bolting and double bolting on the inside.' You don't stop believing the bastard exists; you start believing he hates you.

And part of you is lost in wonder at how peculiar the world looks and feels when it has turned inside out. I was constantly surprised by my own behaviour. I was calm; I didn't howl and scream as some people do. I didn't gather my son's body into my arms. I just dropped one kiss on his hand, and can feel its coldness now; that awful marble chill. No mother on earth should have to know this.

If you ask me how I endured it, I can only say I didn't really; I was numb. My eyes streamed tears until my lids were gravelly and sore. Sometimes I broke out into weird, chesty sobs like a seal barking. But I was numb; I stood beside my son's coffin, stunned by the unreality of everything, knowing what I felt and unable to feel it.

I hated and feared the silence, which had at its centre the raw, gaping absence of Felix. His bedroom was next to mine and for the first few weeks I had to have the World Service waffling through the night to distract me from the screaming quiet. I was physically exhausted, but couldn't escape enough to fall asleep. Instead of counting sheep, I mentally recited the titles of Scott's Waverley novels, usually losing consciousness around number seventeen. Or I did 'This is the House that Jack Built'. I needed the mental noise to drown out all the thoughts that would hurt me, as most of them did. And still do. The pain, when it pounces at you, is quite incredible.

The cosmos has turned its back on you; you feel invisible and somehow rebuked and disgraced. Prayer doesn't help me, if it ever did; I can't even remember what my 'normal' belief felt like. When Felix died, I had a kind of spiritual stroke, and the praying part of my mind is still paralysed.

It's odd that there is so little literature about the weird landscape of grief. There are plenty of pastel-coloured books filled with bad verses and pictures of sunsets, but these are ludicrously inadequate. Consoling verses from the Bible are a mockery and a torment. Tennyson's beautiful *In Memoriam* is too mellow and nostalgic to express the brutality of that first shock. *A Grief Observed*, however, is the most accurate account of bereavement, in all its shock and guilt and pain, that I have ever seen, and reading it made me cry with the relief of not being entirely alone.

I'm particularly grateful to Lewis for putting into words one of my own worst fears: 'to reach a state in which my years of love . . . should appear in retrospect a charming episode – like a holiday – that had briefly interrupted my interminable life'. A single summer, a flash of light; Felix's life passed so quickly. I can't bear to think of his being left behind in the past, while I travel further away from him. I can't bear to think of myself as a sad old woman who once had a son. But that's only self-pity; it's thinking of the life Felix might have had that is most unbearable of all. It makes me want to be dead. God can do anything, so why not that? If he knows me at all, he knows I can't live without my boy.

People talk about the 'stages' of grief – denial, anger, acceptance, whatever – without realising that all the stages are present all the time, and any one of them can attack you at any moment. 'Everything repeats,' Lewis writes. 'The same leg is cut off time after time.' You are Prometheus chained to the rock; your innards are clawed out every afternoon at four, and though it will never get less painful, you eventually learn to factor it into your day.

The first few months after a death are very dark and confused, and when I first read *A Grief Observed* I absorbed only the anguish, angrily skipping the smallest hint of hope when I knew perfectly well there wasn't any. When I came back to it a few months later, however, I was able to see that some of the torments Lewis described are actually small signs of progress, if not recovery.

He notices how 'passionate grief' drives the beloved person further away, and I do remember how hard it became to conjure up an exact picture of Felix in my mind – until the memories started to come back to me, usually when I was thinking about something else. This is a different grade of pain, a couple of notches less savage. I'd have a sudden flash of the sound of his voice, the shape of his eyes, and for a moment he wouldn't feel so absolutely lost to me. I don't want him to turn into a fictional character.

My world is dark and will always be dark. The death of a child is a wound that will never heal, and there's no getting used to hefting round that sack of everlasting sorrow. Lewis again: 'Reality, looked at steadily, is unbearable.'

The kindliness and honesty of Lewis's tone are healing in themselves, and he has taught me to see (or at least begin to see) that just when I thought God had deserted me, there were signs of him everywhere – glaring signs, if I chose to see them. A true believer (I'm still not sure) would say he showed himself through the amazing, radiant kindness of my family and friends. As one old friend put it, the 'goodness' that came out was almost as great a shock as the death.

Nearly two years after I lost Felix, the noise inside my head has calmed down enough for me to listen to the echoes of memories that are kind. The other day I 'heard' my father, a man much given to sayings (both my dear old parents were long dead when Felix died), rolling out one of his favourite quotations: 'If after the manner of men I have fought with beasts at Ephesus, what advantageth it me, if the dead rise not?'

And then I knew he would launch into Mother Julian of Norwich – 'All shall be well, and all shall be well' – to which he would always add, 'And all manner of thing shall be oojah-cum-spiff.'

Francis Spufford

By the time C. S. Lewis published *A Grief Observed*,
under a pseudonym, in 1961, he was the best-known
Christian apologist in the English-speaking world.
He was famous for a printed voice that spoke to his
readers as directly as he had on the radio during the
Blitz, when his reputation was born, and famous too
for his willingness to put the formidable resources of
his learning, imagination and prose style at the service
of ruthless argumentation. Warmly, richly, sometimes
beautifully, he had arm-wrestled his readers towards
belief. He had written a trio of full-length apologetic
works, *Mere Christianity*, *The Problem of Pain* and
Miracles, and many essays; a theological science-fiction
trilogy; the Narnia books for children, with their
underpinning of Christian allegory; and a memoir of
his own conversion, *Surprised by Joy*. He was deeply
admired by some, deeply disliked by others, for his
bullish confidence. *A Grief Observed* is a startling
departure from all this.

It has often been not mis-represented but over-
represented as the book in which C. S. Lewis's faith
breaks down in the face of sorrow: the apologist's creed

being tested by experience, and found wanting. This is not true, at least at the level of ideas. Throughout the dark night of bereavement and despair that the book records, the premises of Lewis's Christianity remain intact. He is much more able to contemplate the possibility that God might be cruel or wicked than that there might be no God, and the idea that God might not be controlling events does not even occur to him. His picture of God darkens for a time into the Cosmic Sadist, and the vet who operates without anaesthetic, but it does not break apart. It does not turn to dust and blow away.

But something has changed, something major that sets this book apart from the rest of his writing, and gives it a power that *Mere Christianity* and *The Problem of Pain* entirely lack, to speak to people who do not share his premises and likely never will. What it is, I think, is that here everything in human experience Lewis names at last has its full weight. Here, sorrow and despair, the tiredness and numbness and petulance and nightmarishness of grief, all have their full, uncontrolled, experienced force, and so their meanings can no longer be taken for granted. Lewis can no longer do what he was often previously inclined to do, in his apologetics, and reason back from the faith-derived interpretation of an event in human life, to reshape the event itself. He cannot indulge in the instinctive over-easy Platonism that, giving priority to the Idea of something, treats all actual instances of it as tidy-able shadows. The quality of eloquent games-playing has vanished from his voice. Now pain hurts, now loss tears holes in the fabric of days and hours. If you are aghast, if you are stunned and becalmed by grief, as Lewis is at the beginning of the book, then neat verbal procedures designed to deal with it by sorting out why break down on the simple discovery that you still are aghast. Argument, as much as common sense, shrivels 'like an ant in the mouth of a furnace'. The fact of pain, not the problem of it, predominates. 'The thing itself is simply all these ups and downs.' Solutions are no longer the point.

Not that Lewis hadn't had a life before his short marriage to Joy Davidman; not that he hadn't suffered before he lost her. His mother had died of cancer when he was a child; he had been a teenage subaltern in the trenches of the Great War; he had nursed along his adoptive family in Oxford for twenty years, until his replacement mother figure (and possibly lover) Janie Moore died as well. The bachelor life he finds he cannot want to return to, in *A Grief Observed*, was a real life. He knew about the fear he compared this new grief to. But in the past he had tended to deal with these things by muffling them, by transposing them into abstraction, or story, or the cut-and-thrust of dialectic. He had dealt with mortality by focusing his attention on the Christian consolation at its most striking, paradoxical and emotionally inconsequential.

Take this (ironically, quite weightless) passage from his 1941 sermon 'The Weight of Glory':

> You have never talked to a mere mortal. Nations, cultures, arts, civilisation – these are mortal, and their life is to ours as the life of a gnat. But it is immortals whom we joke with, work with, marry, snub, and exploit – immortal horrors or everlasting splendours.

Death is trivial. We are more indestructible than the Parthenon. Demigod or Thing with Tentacles: that, gentlemen, is the choice before us. Then compare this:

> I look up at the night sky. Is anything more certain than that in all those vast times and spaces, if I were allowed to search them, I should nowhere find her face, her voice, her touch? She died. She is dead. Is the word so difficult to learn?

The two are perfectly compatible theologically, of course. But not emotionally. One is serious and the other is not; one hoists, on a human back, the weight of all it names, and the other is a charming word game, coloured in by Lewis's mythopoeic imagination.

In *A Grief Observed* Lewis is letting himself feel the

losses of the present moment (and perhaps his accumulated past losses too) without his ancient defences; without the contrivances of mind and imagination, which, like the snowfall onto the image of his wife, would have been worse than the pain. He wanted the reality of loss. He turned to face it, he embraced it, he didn't pretend. Hence the radical openness of the book, set beside his other exercises in memoir and self-description. It lets the permanent loss of faith and meaning be a real possibility, even though Lewis himself does not go that way, in the end. It is too consumed by experience to handle it ruthlessly for the purposes of persuasion, so it can only persuade as another human's experience persuades. It only has the authority of having happened to someone.

It still has elements of performance, naturally. Lewis grief-struck is still Lewis the writer, still incurably a processor of reality through language, with a brilliant eye for the effective move, and a particular weakness for the analogy that creates the illusion of a problem solved. But now he knows it. 'The fruition of God. Re-union with the dead. These can't figure in my thinking except as counters. Blank cheques.' 'And all this time I may, once more, be building with cards.' And the self-possession of the man who, at the end of the book, once more finds himself a believer, has passed through the dispossessing fire, and knows its own incompleteness: its openness to being scorched again, knocked flat again. (Pick your metaphor.) Hence the reader's ability to respect it even if we have arrived somewhere very different. Lewis had always been clever, and in some respects unscrupulous in his use of cleverness. At the end of his life, though, as his friend Austin Farrar said, he became 'a magnificent man'. He had paid the cost to be wise, which is, as ever, both ordinary and extortionate.

Maureen Freely

For as long as I can remember – all my life, almost – I have been fending off death. It's there in every frame: the mushroom cloud on the horizon, the crumbling cliff path, the accident waiting to happen. I could make a strong case for not being alone in this. I am a child of the Cold War, after all. But the dread we all shared – the static nightmare, in which a distant and invisible finger pressing on a distant and invisible button might unleash, without warning, the firestorm that would engulf the world – was in me a dread multiplied, because I was an odd sort of child, who buried herself in books written for adults and took the metaphors in them literally. I also had the good and bad fortune to grow up on the shores of the Bosphorus, and when I watched the Soviet navy passing beneath our balcony, all the hours of the day and night, I would wonder why my parents and their wild, romantic friends refused to take them seriously, when they, like me, had read in *Time* magazine about the marauding bands of communists that might be lurking in the bowels of those ships.

So I made it my mission to watch over them. I kept my eyes on that horizon. Tried to keep them away from cliffs. And when I left home, I took the habit with me. If I loved someone, I was afraid for him. If I loved someone, it was my job to keep him alive.

I loved Frank very much, and I could see, early on, and maybe even the day we met, that his grasp on life was tenuous. I could see also that he was struggling to hang on to that cliff, that on a good day he would find the strength to scramble back to safety. And over the next twenty-five years, most days were good days. But there were also the bad days, when he put himself beyond our reach. And those bad days were very hard to bear.

When I came home that night, I was angry to find him in his study in a stupor. He had been drinking. The vodka bottle in his hands was not yet empty. And so I shouted at him. I told him how I felt. I warned him, as I had done so many times, that he could not go on punishing his body like that. One day it would give out on him. One day I would, too. What I did not know was that this day had already come. Some hours earlier, he'd suffered a stroke.

All our children were with me at the hospital when he died two days later. And many of our friends were there, too. They all said the same thing: you did your best. You did too much, in fact. You cannot blame yourself. I could see their point, though at that point I could also see it was beyond my reach.

All I could see was my own failure. My friends could

see this, too. We're worried for you, they said. You have to look after yourself. And so I promised. I promised to try. I tried very hard, in fact. I had the children to consider, after all. I had to make sure they carried on with their lives. I had to convince them that this was what their father would have wanted. I had to make sure they didn't worry about me unduly. I had to learn how to live alone. But it was hard to live alone, in this rambling cottage at the edge of Bath that we'd been fixing up for years and never finishing, and what about his beautiful terraced garden? How was I to tend it – I who didn't know a thorn from a weed?

I went outside one sunny day and tried to pull up all the dandelions and nearly fainted. I went back inside, to the ghosts that still inhabited each room. I thought about his clothes, and what to do with them. I looked at his briefcase, still leaning against the dining-room wall. I thought about moving it. Move it where? I tried not to think about his shoes, which were still under our bed, which was now, strictly speaking, not our bed. Just mine. But it was still his chair I sat in, when I listened to his music.

I do not believe in God. Actually, it's more serious than that. I was taught not to believe in him, by a father who (when still very young, and long before he found his true vocation in physics) had considered the priesthood. He wanted to spare me the fog of faith, and he was so successful that, even now, when I can see what a blessing faith would be, I cannot bring myself to capitalise that pronoun. There is a blank inside me, where others keep their faith. As much as I would wish it to be otherwise, I simply cannot understand how any rational adult could genuinely believe that God was more than just a metaphor. And that was the crux of my problem when, following a kindly friend's suggestion, I picked up *A Grief Observed*.

The pulsing, all-encompassing swarm of emotions that C. S. Lewis describes in the opening passage: the restlessness, the fluttering stomach, and all the other trappings of fear, the illusion of mild drunkenness, or even concussion, the 'invisible blanket' that seemed to divide him from the world around him – all these I recognised. Just as I recognised the clean, clear moments of agony – so much more honest than those long hours of lazy but suspenseful circular thinking, the impatience with imperfect photographs, or the descent into 'maudlin tears'. What made no sense to me was the question that makes its first appearance in the seventh paragraph and dominates the rest of the book: 'Meanwhile, where is God?'

What did he mean by this question? What was lurking underneath? Mystified, I carried on reading, while he raged against his cruel God, and I struggled with his metaphors.

Until one night he had a dream he could describe only in figures of speech. 'Imagine a man in total darkness,' he suggested. 'He thinks he's in a cellar or a dungeon. Then there comes a sound. He thinks it might be a sound from far off – waves or wind-blown trees or cattle half a mile away. And if so, it proves he's not in a cellar, but free, in the open air. Or it may be a much smaller sound close at hand – a chuckle of laughter. And if so, there is a friend just beside him in the dark.' He was, he said, not mad enough to take this as proof of anything. He was, quite simply, transcribing an act of the imagination, an acknowledgement that any of us might be utterly mistaken 'as to the situation he is really in'. It did not feel like love, he said. But it felt very intimate, and so, too, did the recollection with which he ended the book: his beloved H, on her deathbed, turning away from him, and towards eternity.

I've travelled across three continents since losing Frank. I've written or translated hundreds of thousands of words. I've finished the work on the house that Frank once despaired of ever finishing. I've convinced all our children that I'm thriving. But his briefcase is still where he left it. On my evenings at home, I still sit in his chair, listening to his music. Sometimes, while I'm listening, I pick up this book to look again, to read about the dream, which is really more of a metaphor, or an act of imagination transcribed: the man in total darkness, the sound that might be waves or wind-blown trees, or could be a friend standing next to him, gently chuckling. And sometimes, just sometimes – after I've put the book away, and closed my eyes, to let the music back in – I can imagine Frank next to me, sharing the night.

About the Authors

HILARY MANTEL's most recent book is *The Assassination of Margaret Thatcher: Stories*. She has twice won the Man Booker prize, for her novels *Wolf Hall* and *Bring Up the Bodies*.

JESSICA MARTIN is an Anglican parish priest serving the three villages of Duxford, Hinxton and Ickleton in South Cambridgeshire, and an Honorary Canon of Ely Cathedral. Before that she was for ten years Fellow and College Lecturer in English at Trinity College, Cambridge. Recent publications include *John Milton's Paradise Lost: How to Believe* (2013), a Kindle 'Guardian Short' originally run in the online *Guardian* in 2011, and (with Alec Ryrie), *Private and Domestic Devotion in Early Modern England* (Ashgate, 2012).

JENNA BAILEY is a writer and social historian. She has her PhD in Contemporary History from the University of Sussex and is currently the Visiting Research Fellow for the Centre for Life History and Life Writing Research (CLHLWR) at the University of Sussex and an Executive Member of the Centre for Oral History and Tradition (COHT) at the University of Lethbridge, Canada. Jenna is the author of the bestselling *Can Any Mother Help Me?* (Faber & Faber) and is currently working on her next book about Ivy Benson's All Girl Band.

ROWAN WILLIAMS grew up in South Wales, studied theology at Cambridge and did research in Oxford into Russian religious philosophy. He has worked as a parish priest and university teacher, becoming Bishop of Monmouth in 1992 and Archbishop of Canterbury in 2002. He retired from this office in 2012 and is now Master of C. S. Lewis's Cambridge college, Magdalene. He has written many books on theology and social and political questions including a study of C. S. Lewis's Narnia fantasies and a series of Gifford Lectures, *The Edge of Words* (Continuum 2014); he has also published several books of poetry, most recently *The Other Mountain* (Carcanet 2014).

KATE SAUNDERS is a full-time author and journalist and has written numerous novels including *The Marrying Game* and *Bachelor Boys*. Her books for children have won awards and received enthusiastic reviews, and include future classics such as *Beswitched* and *The Whizz Pop Chocolate Shop*. Her latest novel for children, *Five Children on the Western Front*, is a sequel to E. Nesbit's

Five Children and It stories and takes place in 1914 on the eve of the First World War. Kate lives in London.

FRANCIS SPUFFORD has published five books with Faber & Faber, the second of which, *The Child that Books Built*, included a long reckoning with his childhood love for the Narnia books, while the most recent, *Unapologetic*, was an attempt at a sort of plausible counterpart to Lewis's apologetics, suitable for contemporary Britain. He teaches at Goldsmiths College, University of London.

MAUREEN FREELY is the author of seven novels; the most recent, *Sailing through Byzantium*, was published in 2013. She has translated several books by the Turkish Nobel Laureate, Orhan Pamuk, as well as other twentieth century and contemporary works. Currently the President of English PEN, she teaches at the University of Warwick.

ff

Faber and Faber is one of the great independent publishing houses. We were established in 1929 by Geoffrey Faber with T. S. Eliot as one of our first editors. We are proud to publish award-winning fiction and non-fiction, as well as an unrivalled list of poets and playwrights. Among our list of writers we have five Booker Prize winners and twelve Nobel Laureates, and we continue to seek out the most exciting and innovative writers at work today.

Find out more about our authors and books
faber.co.uk

Read our blog for insight and opinion on books and the arts
thethoughtfox.co.uk

Follow news and conversation
twitter.com/faberbooks

Watch readings and interviews
youtube.com/faberandfaber

Connect with other readers
facebook.com/faberandfaber

Explore our archive
flickr.com/faberandfaber